Harmonic Messaging

Bonnie Mauldin
2023.

Harmonic Messaging

Make Your Brand, Sales & Marketing Sing in Harmony

Bonnie Mauldin

ISBN: 978-1-7353185-2-3 - Paperback
ISBN: 978-1-7353185-6-1 - Hardcover
eISBN: 978-1-7353185-3-0 - eBook

Library of Congress Control Number: 2023901829

♾This paper meets the requirements of ANSI/NISO Z39.48-1992 (Permanence of Paper)

Front cover photograph by Drea Nicole Photography, LLC.
Back cover photograph by Mike Glatzer Photography

Printed in the United States of America 0 2 0 2 2 3

CONTENTS

INTRODUCTION

Zero. Zilch. Nada . . . that's the number of leads I received from my first marketing campaign. It had taken me six months to save $1,500 from my nine-to-five job so I could start a wellness coaching business.

I hired this guy to run paid ads for me, and he promised me the moon and stars. It was so exciting to dream about all the new clients I could serve after the campaign started, but the dream turned into a nightmare after I realized that no clients were coming and I had completely waisted my money—and time.

This put me on a path to start studying digital advertising. It was during the time when platforms like Google and Facebook were taking off, early 2000s. I was hooked; after learning how to optimize a page to show up on the first page of Google, and post messages on Facebook to get people to show up at my events, I knew I found my life's calling.

I love business—every aspect of starting, marketing, and growing a business. And one thing I could do to be around business all the time was to start a marketing agency to help others build and grow their companies as *I had done for my own.*

So, it's been over fifteen years since the day I lost the $1,500 that I had diligently saved for six months. Now I know how to run paid ads, social media campaigns, search engine optimization, and content marketing. My love for music and business helped me see the correlations between being in a band and building a brand. So that's how this book came about . . .

After helping hundreds of business owners and companies get new customers, I've learned a thing or two about what works and what does not. Harmonic Messaging is all about how to *make your brand, sales, and marketing work harmoniously together*.

After reading this book, you'll be able to:

- Create a profitable sales and marketing strategy
- Build lead-generating websites and advertising campaigns
- Implement an exceptional branding program to raise awareness and build credibility

Many small-to-mid-sized companies have just one or two people performing marketing tasks, and this leaves multiple areas of marketing totally neglected. There is misalignment for brand message, sales message, and online presence when there is no strategic plan in place to express core values at every touchpoint.

I've remedied this problem with a five-phase framework I call "Harmonic Messaging" (HM). My HM philosophy is all about bringing out the very best in a company's story, unique selling points, features, benefits, and personnel to make the company stand out in a crowd of competition.

Our clients experience a customized, tailormade (harmonic) message that resonates with ideal clients. This, in turn, improves the quality of leads, improves the effectiveness of sales, and ultimately improves profits of the company in an extraordinary way.

My Harmonic Message framework is applied to:

- Staff training
- Elevator pitchs
- Sales presentations
- Events: tradeshows, conferences, webinars
- Print collateral
- Websites
- SEO
- PPC
- Social media
- Business listings
- Blogs
- Emails
- Videos
- Public Relations

On average this approach has delivered the following results for our clientele in healthcare, education, construction, manufacturing, real estate, and senior living industries:

- 50 percent increase in website traffic
- 50 percent increase in social media engagement
- 50 percent increase in (high-quality) inbound leads

Give me a call to discuss how this approach might work for you.

Or book me to teach on the following topics:

- Business Development 101
- Social Media Marketing Mastery

- Modern Marketing for Dominating New Markets

As in classical music, where musicians must play the notes that come on sheet music and carefully follow the conductor's directions to perform with the utmost precision to dazzle the audience, our company must work with the same harmony and accuracy to achieve excellence and reach our customers in an everlasting, indelible way. We don't just want to sell, we want to build a relationship, a trust, a friendship.

Throughout this book we will try to explain in an exhaustive way what the HM method consists of, how to apply it to your marketing strategy, how to adapt this strategy to the customer's journey, how to use this harmonization to expand your business, and finally, how to harmonize and integrate two of the departments that clash the most in a company: sales and marketing. Tune your strings because this is going to start rocking immediately. Let's get started!

Learn more at www.harmonicmessaging.com.

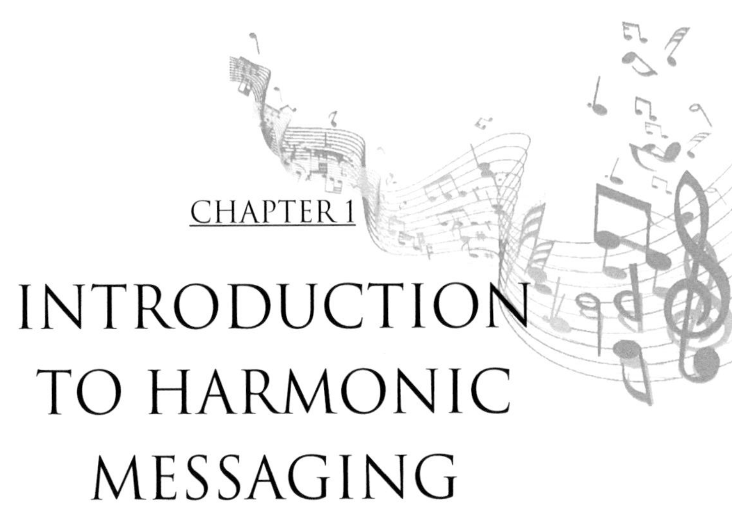

CHAPTER 1

INTRODUCTION TO HARMONIC MESSAGING

> *Harmony makes small things grow; lack of it makes great things decay.*
>
> —Sallust

Communication. A vital tool for everyday life, and even more crucial for a healthy relationship, both personal and business. Yet it is such a complicated concept. When it comes to making your brand, or your business, resonate, you don't just have to worry about using the right tone of voice. You also have to think about using the right channels, methods, and strategies to get your message across.

A brand is more than a name and a logo. Your brand is the holistic perception of your company. It is the recognition of your business entity that helps you differentiate yourself from your competition. In today's oversaturated and overwhelmed marketing environment, building the right reputation for your brand is harder than ever. There are so many communication channels to choose from, from apps to online content to radio and print. That means that if you want to access most of the market and develop a truly effective brand, you have to learn how to integrate your message into a single communicative entity that is a living representation of your brand's personality.

One mistake can be enough to turn your entire communication strategy into a game of Telephone, where your message gets diluted down or changed, as it goes from one person to the next. This can damage your brand's reputation, and reduce your ability to connect with your customers. If you want to take your market share today, you need to know how to harmonize your communications strategies, to achieve the most coherent, seamless and risk-free connections.

Harmonic marketing communications are your company's strategies that focus on controlling the use of language, messages, and images. By harmonizing all aspects of your communications strategy, you build a stronger, more persistent "feel" for your brand, whether you are writing a blog, shooting a video, or publishing a company report.

With a disciplined approach to harmonious marketing communications, you can work to make your brand a household name, increase the chances of cross-pollination between marketing strategies, increase sales, and deliver a better customer experience. In other words, this technique can give small businesses the opportunity to boost their branding and marketing strategies and become market leaders.

If we look at traditional approaches to marketing communications, most agencies and companies plan separate campaigns for press releases, advertising, sales promotions, and direct marketing services. In other words, they get everything they need, but their strategies don't all vibrate to the same beat.

By cultivating a harmonious communication strategy that is respected throughout your brand, you can bring together the same communication tools to reinforce each other and increase effectiveness. Because they all play the same song, supporting the same message and image, your harmonic communications reinforce your brand in advertising and in the eyes of your customers.

WHAT EXACTLY IS HARMONIC MESSAGING?

Harmonic: pertaining to harmony, as distinguished from melody and rhythm; marked by harmony; in harmony; concordant; consonant; physics: of, relating to, or noting a series of oscillations in which each oscillation has a frequency that is an integral multiple of the same basic frequency.

Messaging: a system or process of transmitting messages, especially electronically, by computer, telephone, television cable, etc.

Yes, Harmonic Messaging. We adopted this concept to define an integral strategy and method that helps us to make each of the parts of our advertising machinery vibrate to the same rhythm. If we want to be successful in our communication strategy, we must make all the component parts work together like an orchestra, vibrating at the same frequency set by the director, which in our case will be the mission of our brand. Therefore, we will define our HM as **the strategy that encompasses each and every part of your brand under the same beat, making all parts of your company's messaging work in harmony with each other, to create a beautiful song like an orchestra leading to better brand recognition, increased leads, increased sales, and profitability.**

"Harmonic Messaging" may be a concept that seems complicated at first glance, but it's a lot simpler than you might think. The truth is that it all comes down to making sure you maintain the same image, personality, and voice, regardless of where your brand is located and its objectives.

Basically, it's the difference between having a chaotic brand that is difficult for your target market to relate to and a **consistent company with a strong and deliberate personality**.

With a harmonious communication plan, you ensure that all the information your brand shares is consistent with your brand identity and brand manifesto. To do this, you bring together all your promotional tools and communication strategies into a "brand set."

With a brand set, you can make sure that all the marketing elements of your company play the same song, following the **four Cs of brand harmony**:

- **Coherence**: all communications connect logically.
- **Communication**: all your brand messages support each other.
- **Continuity**: consistency; connect across all spaces.
- **Complementarity**: each aspect of your marketing plan supports the others.

Instead of having different plans for your sales

promotions, press releases, and content marketing, harmonious communications allow you to tie everything together for better results.

Harmonic communications are the "holistic medicine" of marketing. They focus on making sure you maintain a consistent approach both online and offline, regardless of the channel you use. If used correctly, they can build trust with your customers, reinforce your brand presence, and give you a huge advantage over your competitors. Throughout the following chapters, we will delve into the different techniques and steps to take to adopt this strategy holistically. However, during this first chapter, we will start by understanding the first and most important step of all when starting to build your HM strategy: defining who you are, what you do, why you do it, and who you do it for. Let's get started.

DEVELOPING A BRAND IDENTITY

To market anything—a product, a person, an organization, or an idea—you first need to define your brand. Once you establish it, you can create a foundation for all of your marketing efforts and strategies. The definition of your brand will serve as a yardstick against which to evaluate each and every marketing material, from your logo to the color of your business cards.

Think of your brand identity as the way your audience perceives you: it is the face of your company. It is the music sheet that will set the tempo and tone of your song so that all the members of the band can give a good performance. Without a complete and well-defined brand identity, your audience may not understand who you are; your music has to move the listener, and to do that you have to play the right notes. In the end, you have to establish a personal connection. Think of Wal-Mart, identified as your trusted shop. At the time of this writing, they even have people who greet customers as they enter the shop.

It is important to note that brand identity is not the same as branding; brand identity is the product of effective branding.

Brand identity includes aspects such as:

- Your visual identity
- The voice you use
- The value of your brand and your business
- The type of personality you have

All four of these elements come together to create the unique look and tone you want your business to project to the world. **As your business evolves over time, so will your brand identity**. However, you need to create a baseline, a profile that defines who you are, right from the start. Before we start the process, let's look at some key elements to consider:

1. **Know How You Help the Customer Solve a Problem**

Your customers are often interested in your company's product or service because they have a problem that needs solving. For example, you have created a personal finance software program that helps consumers avoid overdrawing their bank accounts. Your customers need you because of an existing problem.

It is imperative that your brand identity immediately tells the customer how you can help them solve a problem (or what is known as a "**pain point**"). Ask yourself whether you offer peace of mind (if you sell alarms) or a convenient way to deliver office supplies to the customer's home. Whatever you offer, the problem you solve should be the cornerstone of your brand identity.

2. What Five Words Describe You?

Here's an exercise that will help you define your brand identity, and it won't take long. Sit down (preferably with a group of five or six people) and draw up a list of the five adjectives that most describe your brand personality. It is important that the list does not exceed six adjectives, otherwise you will not focus on your personality.

A good way to start is to think about what drove the CEO or founder of your company in the first place. Those are the things that drive your business.

Questions to Ask Yourself

Once you have addressed the most important aspects, you need to ask yourself the following questions:

- What are the specific qualities of the services and/or products you offer? Make sure you are as specific as possible. For example, don't say you offer public relations services. Say you are a public relations specialist with expertise in traditional and digital media relations.
- What are the core values of your products and services? What are the core values of your company? When thinking about values, think about what is most important to you and your customers. This is especially important for non-profit organizations.

- What is your company's mission? This is often a question of ethics and standards.
- What does your company specialize in? That is, what is your niche? For example, if you sell gift baskets, perhaps you specialize in Christmas gift baskets or cheese and fruit gift baskets.
- Who is your target audience? This involves identifying the people who are attracted to your products and services. For example, if you are targeting older people, this is a very well-defined and age-specific audience.
- What is your company's slogan and what kind of message does your slogan send to your potential customers? Not every organization has a slogan, but if you want one, keep it very short.

Once you have answered the first six questions, create a personality for your company that clearly represents your products or services. Ask yourself what qualities differentiate you from the competition—is your company's personality innovative, traditional, practical, creative, energetic, or sophisticated? Create a profile for your brand. Describe the personality by choosing words you would use when writing your biography or explaining to a colleague why your business is unique. Be creative.

Let's give you some more ideas:

Does Your Brand Have an Emotional Impact?

If you pay attention to what your new, satisfied customers are saying about you, you can learn a lot about your brand's ability to connect with your customer base.

What you need to know is how it makes your customers feel.

Your brand can produce any of the following emotions:

- *Comfort*
- *Safety*
- *Well-being*
- *Creativity*
- *Loneliness*
- *Benevolence*
- *Inspiration*
- *Relevance*

If, for example, a preponderance of customers say they feel relevant, that is critical information that will help you build a brand identity.

DEFINE YOUR MISSION, VISION, AND VALUES

The vision, mission, and values of a company are its DNA or corporate identity, which gives it coherence, authenticity, and originality as a brand. Currently, there is too much haste in the process of creating a company or business and the need to define these three basic concepts is overlooked, but this step is fundamental to finish building our brand identity and to set the beat of the song we will perform for our customers.

As well as defining these aspects, it is important to have a SWOT (Strengths, Weaknesses, Opportunities, Threats) analysis as a continuous feedback tool, as it allows the company's strategy to be clearly identified.

HOW TO DEFINE THE MISSION, VISION, AND VALUES OF A COMPANY

To be an entrepreneur or business owner, you must have, at least, a clear mission and vision for your company and, based on this, you must be able to grow your business. The importance of knowing how to correctly develop the vision and mission is fundamental, as these will help us to create new, innovative, and important goals in order to become what we want to be.

Any company that wants to be successful and seek profits must undergo a formal system of strategic management—that is, select and perfectly define its values within the value chain of the company that will make it stand out from the competition.

Strategic management can be divided into three phases:

1. **Defining strategic objectives.**
    - Defining the philosophy and mission of the company or business unit.
    - Setting short- and long-term objectives to achieve the company's mission, which defines the present and future business activities of an organization.
2. **Strategic planning.**
    - Formulating various possible strategies and choosing the one that will be most appropriate to achieve the objectives set out in the company's mission.
    - Developing an organizational structure to achieve the strategy.
3. **Strategic implementation.**
    - Ensuring the activities necessary to ensure that the strategy is delivered effectively.

- Monitor the effectiveness of the strategy in achieving the organization's objectives.

What Is a Company's Mission?

A company's mission describes the activity and identity that is key to the organization's achievement of its vision, which are the goals or accomplishments that constitute the purpose of the company's existence. It is the fundamental reason and goal of a company or business always seen in the long term.

The concept of mission is fundamental and must be fully aligned with the vision of the future we want to achieve. A simple way to explain what the mission is would be to find the answer to the why.

Here are a series of questions to help you shape the mission of a company:

- What do you want to offer?
- Why do you want to create this business?
- What is the user profile you want to attract?
- What business image do you want to communicate?
- What factors determine the price and quality of your products and/or services?
- What relationship will you have with your employees?
- What is your differentiating aspect that makes you stand out from your competitors?
- Can your business really be competitive?

Having found the answers to these and other questions, we will be able to get closer to the fundamental reasons why we have created this business and what are the objectives we want to achieve.

What Is a Company's Vision?

Defined by Jack Fleitman in his book *Successful Businesses* (McGraw Hill, 2000) as *"the path toward which the company is heading in the long term and serves as a direction and incentive to guide strategic decisions for growth and competitiveness."*

The vision of a company could be called the DREAM. It is a statement of the company's aspirations in the medium or long term; it is the future image of what we want the company to be like in the future. Its purpose is to be the driving force and guide the organization to achieve the desired state.

It starts from drawing on a piece of paper the current state of your business and then draw the future image of it.

In short, it is about finding out what we need to achieve in order to ensure the sustainability and growth of the business. As we did with the mission, we leave you with a series of questions to help you shape the vision of your company:

- What will your company look like in a few years?
- What are your short-, medium-, and long-term goals?
- What will be the key values and attitudes of the company?
- What do you want people to think of your company in the future?
- What aspects of growth would you like to achieve?

Whenever we work on a business plan, we should always be able to draw how we would like to see our business in two and four years' time, but bear in mind that a plan is never a static and fixed element, but rather an element that must grow and vary according to the evolution of the company.

How to Define the Values of a Company?

This intangible asset, which is so important at the same time, helps us to define the ethical principles of our company or business.

A company with values attracts and retains professional talent, which leads to more sales and better results. The question then is: how do you define them? **How do you attach values to a company's corporate philosophy?** Which values fit best with what we do? Let's take these five steps as a reference:

1. *Define the things that are important to your business.*

You can start by making a list of the most important things for your business. For example, if you are in the courier and parcel business, punctuality, responsibility, and speed should certainly be on the list. These things are almost always defined in terms of the customer or internal processes that we consider essential to achieve results.

2. *Prioritize.*

From this list it is necessary to highlight the most significant items. Remember that not everything in a business is equally important. Speed may be the most valuable element for you, while another company that does the same thing may prefer to prioritize accountability. That's what it's all about—knowing what matters most to us as a company.

3. *Reduce or eliminate contradictions.*

Look closely at your priorities. You may find contradictions in them that can cause problems in defining your corporate values. Eliminate them or reduce them as much as possible. Remember that values cannot cancel each other out or create ambiguity. Corporate philosophy is expressed through a compact, solid, and coherent discourse.

4. *Habits that support the priorities.*

The next step is to determine what daily habits or practices can help us to promote the values we have chosen. We may come up with a lot of ideas. But it may also happen that a certain value cannot be implemented because it is inconsistent with the organizational model. This also needs to be taken into account.

5. *Identify distinctive features.*

Finally, another way of identifying the most appropriate corporate values is by looking at those elements, aspects, or features that make us different from other companies in the market. For example, if we have the most advanced technology in the sector, a value that may go hand in hand with this will be the efficiency of the processes. Distinctive features, also known as competitive advantages, become assets if we know how to exploit them to our advantage.

Whatever area of performance or productive activity you want to enter into, be sure to go through these steps. Corporate values are much more than mere concepts, they are the ones that express your way of understanding business.

Haven't you ever come across a company where everyone seems to be going in a different direction? Well, those are classic cases of businesses that do not have company values that are well marked or respected by their members. It is really like having a symphony orchestra without a conductor, where each one plays the song as he/she feels like, but without coordinating with the others.

Here are some really positive aspects of having, applying, fostering, and transmitting company values:

- Creating a strong and solid organizational culture
- Encouraging staff to help with the company's objectives
- Achieving low staff turnover
- Avoiding differences of opinion among employees
- Clear perspective and change thinking for new talent
- Providing the opportunity to deliver and contribute in settings that are aligned with the company's values and having a presence in corporate social responsibility campaigns
- To build trust and credibility with customers, suppliers, employees, etc.
- In order for each member to feel a sense of belonging to the company, you must create an environment full of values!

Let us review the essential values that every company should have.

1. **Honesty**

Transparency, sincerity, and openness are values that the public today not only wants from companies but demands from them. This has to do with using the truth as a tool to gain trust and credibility with the environment.

2. **Quality**

We live in a world where everyone claims to have the best products on the market. But it is one thing to claim it and another to guarantee it. Products must meet the established and promised parameters, which can only be close to perfection.

3. **Punctuality**

We are not only talking about being respectful with the delivery times of goods, we also attach importance to punctuality at the time of arrival and departure. Also, have special consideration for the time of customers, suppliers, and partners in cases of meetings and payment of invoices.

4. **Passion**

Few things attract customers more than seeing people who enjoy what they do. Therefore, having passion as a company value will serve to create and keep the emotionality at the top and transmit that motivation to the outside.

5. **Competitiveness**

Having the clear goal that you can only be satisfied being at the top is a value that very few manage to put into practice. Your company can only be the best if you demand the best. When this happens, morale, passion, and motivation will never be lacking, and the growth of the organization is a natural consequence.

6. Teamwork

When have you ever seen a sports team win championships on the basis of individuals alone? Possibly never. Team management emerges as an important necessity in corporate environments where tolerance, respect, admiration, and consideration are priorities. In the end, the success of a song depends on everyone's contribution. Everyone must actively participate and do their part.

But it does not stop there, the values of a company are linked to the personal principles of the heads of the company. Therefore, values such as freedom, resilience, loyalty, solidarity, among others, can also be considered.

7. Customer orientation

A company that constantly strives to rethink its value proposition to suit the needs of its customers has everything it needs to grow sustainably. In the end, businesses only continue to exist because their consumers choose them to solve a problem or gap, based on products and services. In other words, the customer is the backbone of a successful business.

That is why customer orientation brings so many benefits to corporate processes. This value can be incorporated into the organizational culture with the following measures:

- Implement a customer-success department
- Define clear goals and OKRs (Objectives and Key Results)
- Conducting interviews with current and potential customers to understand their perceptions
- Personalizing offers
- Use artificial intelligence tools to generate data on customer-company interactions
- Map the touchpoints of the customer journey
- Promote effective customer experience actions

8. Social responsibility

Taking into account the previous point, the role of companies in improving the quality of life of people, starting with their customers, is clear. But this movement can be further strengthened when it is extended to the community at large.

In order to have a broad and positive impact on the society around them, businesses must give strength to the value of social responsibility. That is, they can take collective action to make their resources work for the benefit of people who do not necessarily have a consumer relationship with them.

Some examples of this process are:

- Financial and structural support to non-profit institutions that act in causes of interest to the company
- Creation of educational courses and workshops to pass on the knowledge it produces

- Support for small entrepreneurs to stimulate their growth in the market
- Development of a free and more limited version of a software or app for those who cannot afford the main product

9. Problem-solving

When entering the corporate world, it is best to remove the illusion that you can build a perfect scenario without any problems. This is impossible because in the attempt to grow and improve, limitations arise that the company must overcome.

This is why the value of problem-solving is so important in the business environment. Employees and managers should always encourage solution-oriented thinking, thus avoiding wasting time finding fault or regretting what didn't work.

This is one of the pillar values of the organizational culture of a successful brand. They do this with interesting and effective resources, such as:

- Constant alignment meetings between managers and analysts, in a 1:1 (one on one) format;
- Dialogue spaces for brainstorming ideas and solutions to identified errors;
- Application of the PDCA (Plan, Do, Check, Act) methodology, which seeks the root cause of each problem;
- . . . among others.

10. Capacity for analysis and self-criticism

All companies must carry out regular analyses that allow them to discover their strengths and weaknesses to know what mistakes they have made in the past and must not make again. One of the biggest mistakes companies make is to think that they are always right and that their strategy is the right one. However, self-criticism is capable of detecting mistakes in time that, in the long run, can be very costly.

Now that you have the keys to define the vision, mission, and values of your brand, let's look at some practical examples that will help you to understand it all better and to see the importance of a good description of these elements in order to consolidate your company as a success among your customers. These elements will help you understand which notes to play to create a harmonious, tuneful song that resonates effectively on all channels.

Some examples of great companies in relation to the terms mission, vision, and values can be analyzed here:

››› Coca-Cola's Mission, Vision, and Values

Example of a Company Mission

It is the long-term objective of the Coca-Cola Company, and it is also the main criterion when making important decisions and actions for the brand in order to achieve three fundamental goals:

- Refresh the world.
- Inspire moments of optimism and happiness.
- Create value and make a difference.

Example of a Company Vision

It is the framework of the business plan and describes

what needs to be achieved to achieve maximum sustainability, quality, and growth. It aims to achieve objectives tailored to different areas:

- People: to be a good place to work, so that people feel inspired to give the best of themselves every day.
- Beverages: to offer a varied portfolio of quality products that anticipate and satisfy the desires and needs of consumers.
- Partners: develop a network to create common and lasting value.
- Planet: be a responsible citizen who makes a difference by helping to build and support sustainable communities.
- Profit: maximize returns to shareholders while being mindful of the company's overall responsibilities.
- Productivity: be an efficient and dynamic organization.

EXAMPLE OF A COMPANY'S VALUES

They guide the actions and behavior of the Coca-Cola Company around the world and are:

- Leadership: striving to shape a better future.
- Collaboration: to leverage collective talent.
- Integrity: being transparent.
- Accountability: being responsible.
- Passion: to be committed with heart and mind.
- Diversity: have a wide range of brands and be as inclusive as they are.
- Quality: striving for excellence.

››› Nike's Mission, Vision, and Values

VISION

To bring inspiration and innovation to every athlete on the planet.

MISSION

To be the largest retailer of shoes and apparel for athletes in the world.

> "Representation and reliability of shoes, apparel, and equipment, new product development, pricing, product identity across the marketplace and promotion as well as customer service and support are important aspects of competency in the tennis, apparel, and sports equipment industry . . . we believe we are competitive in all of these areas."

The company's goal is to "give the corporate employee advantage through proactive programs that reflect care for the global Nike family; our teammates, our customers and those who provide services to Nike."

››› Google's Mission, Vision, and Values

VISION

Google was born with the vision of organizing all the information on the internet so that it is available to everyone.

In fact, the name Google is a mathematical play on words that comes from the mathematical term "googol," which refers to a one followed by one hundred zeros, symbolizing the large amount of information on the internet.

MISSION

To achieve its vision, Google has three main missions, which arise from the three types of audiences it has (the users of its search engine, those who produce the information, and businesses):

- To show the most relevant and reliable information available.
- Help content creators to get more visibility.
- Offer an advertising platform accessible to all.

VALUES

Among its most outstanding values are:

- Speed
- Innovation
- Accuracy
- Usability
- Impartiality

››› NETFLIX'S MISSION, VISION, AND VALUES

VISION

Netflix's vision is to entertain the world by offering its customers the best platform where they can watch the series, movies, and documentaries they love, whenever they want, wherever they want, without ads.

MISSION

To achieve its vision, Netflix has three main missions, which arise from the three types of audience it has: users of its streaming service, those who produce information, and companies.

- To offer the best content.
- To keep up to date with technological innovations.
- Be profitable for investors.
- Produce new original and exclusive content for customers.

VALUES

The most important company values for which Netflix stands out the most are:

- Impact
- Passion
- Innovation
- Curiosity
- Inclusiveness
- Communication

As you can see, big companies always have a clearly defined strategic backbone to function and make all the different organs and elements of the company work in relation to it. I hope that this section will encourage you to shape these three key aspects—the mission, vision, and values of your company—and thus define this important corporate identity, which will help you to make the best decisions in the future.

This analysis will be useful for your SWOT analysis of the company, as well as the personal SWOT analysis of all employees.

TELL YOUR BRAND STORY TO THE WORLD

A company's history may seem a minor issue in building its image, but it can play an important role in gaining the trust and respect of customers.

Every company's history is unique. It may have a past full of interesting anecdotes, decisions, or strokes of luck that have defined it as it is today. Many companies have an "About Us" section, but that section can be "generic"—it sends a positive message about the company, but does not convey its essence.

WHAT ARE THE PARTS OF A GOOD COMPANY STORY?

Although every company's story is unique, it is common for all companies to have some key elements in common.

First, all companies have a set of values and a purpose for which they were founded, as we have seen earlier. These were the first driving force in the development of the company. As time goes on, if the company is doing well, there is usually also a defined vision for the future, with clear goals to be achieved. If you have followed the previously mentioned steps and have already defined your brand identity and the mission, vision, and values of your brand, writing your story should be a piece of cake.

HISTORY IS PART OF THE COMPANY'S IMAGE

It is also important to talk about the company's successes. Apart from being a source of pride, it is good to communicate the goals achieved and explain how they are the fruit of good work. This not only gives the company a good image in the eyes of customers but can also be a good way to keep morale high among employees.

On the other hand, it is also good not to hide possible failures. Placed in the right light, they can be taught as a source of learning as well as serving as a means of empathy and rapprochement with customers.

WHY IS A COMPANY'S HISTORY VALUABLE?

A good company story lends credibility to customer-facing advertisements, helps build a clear company image and values, and is also a good tool to approach customers and begin to gain their trust.

A company is a constantly evolving organism. If its story is communicated effectively, it becomes a tool to guide the company's future, attract talent, and reach out to customers.

TIPS FOR WRITING YOUR BRAND STORY

Grab a piece of paper, get inspired, and write:

- How your story began.
- What was that peak moment when you felt the need to bring to life that project you had so much in mind?
- What difficulties you had (if any) in that initial stage.
- What was the "why" and how did you find the "why" and the "how"?
- What things have changed since you started your project?
- How you see yourself in a few years.
- Some anecdotes or memories that come to mind.

A SUCCESS STORY OR POSITIVE TESTIMONIAL THAT YOU CAN TELL

Everyone loves testimonials and, even more so, success stories. So if you have a customer whose life has been improved or changed by your product, there's no better story to tell.

Dove Beauty brand shows the experience of real women who tell their stories in a space dedicated to them, because what matters is not to be perfect but to be natural and to love ourselves as we are.

Dust off the memory boot and the customer file—do you have a customer who has recently benefited from your product or service?

Write:

- How did you meet them?
- What was their situation?
- What was their process?
- What were their struggles to achieve their goal?
- What were their initial fears?
- What were the things that made them believe in your brand?
- What is their life like today?

Ask them to write down, in their own words, what kind of experience your product offered them, what need it filled, and what things in their life work the way they wanted them to today.

WHAT IF YOU DON'T HAVE ANY CLIENTS YET?

If you have just started and you don't have any customers yet, look for a person among your acquaintances who has the profile of your potential customer. Maybe a friend, a friend of a friend, or a relative who is going through that situation, and describe what their current situation is and what their life could be like if they had the opportunity to have your product or service.

HARMONIZING YOUR INTERNAL COMMUNICATIONS

STAFF IS ON THE SAME PAGE AS THE COMPANY

Most companies are beginning to see the importance of defining the mission, vision, and values of the company but they still think that it is for show to post it on the website so that all customers or potential customers can read it. And this is correct; it is important to communicate it to all the stakeholders of the company—customers, suppliers, collaborators, etc. But it is even more important to have communicated it to the employees in a way that they feel involved in it. In the end, the success of a performance depends on everyone's contribution. Everyone must actively participate and do their part, and your staff more than anyone else. This results in spontaneous and beautiful, harmonic teamwork.

We propose a way of communicating it through a simple dynamic where employees are brought together and asked to contribute ideas on how they can contribute to the mission and vision of the company and how making it happen can contribute to their professional and personal development. In this way they will know how their work contributes to the fulfilment of the mission and vision of their company and they will be committed and motivated to make it happen.

Core values are the foundation of every strong business. Just look at the name—*core,* meaning the central or most important part of something, and *values,* the regard that something is held to deserve; the importance, worth, or usefulness of something. Your entire organization should not only have solid core values, but they should hire, fire, review, and reward on these as well.

So how does this apply to company-wide training? Here are a few tips you can implement into your training process to make sure your core values remain as the focal point for your organization.

Keys to Transmitting Corporate Values

From what has been said so far, it is not difficult to deduce the importance of controlling (knowing and defining) the corporate values that make up the culture of an organization. Part of this control is also to ensure their successful transmission, and for this reason I dare to suggest some keys to take into account when carrying out this task. If culture determines behavior and values shape culture . . . watch out what we transmit!

1. Although strictly speaking it is something prior to transmission, values that are not clear and well defined cannot be successfully disseminated. This means making sure that we have not stated them in a way that makes them interpretable or susceptible to being understood through the prism of individual subjectivity. If we have to spend time explaining corporate values, they are not well defined.
2. Connect the inside with the outside. Employees

need to hear the same messages that are sent outward in order to feel motivated. It is not so much an aspect of form as of content. Too often, internal and external communication work in isolation. To build a brand, it is necessary to align marketing, sales, and human resources. In addition to planning and executing internal communication strategies, it is advisable to organize training programs that facilitate the understanding and integration of employees according to described objectives.

3. Whether you are outsourcing your training or handling it in-house, the curriculum is going to be the most important factor in whether or not your employees are engaged in the process. Work with your instructional designer or whoever is handling the training to ensure that your core values are weaved in throughout the process and that there are plenty of tie-ins for your organization. This will help you also niche down your training and make it more relatable to your team, rather than just supplying them with cookie-cutter curriculum that is broad and lacking in sustenance.
4. Take advantage of e-learning and training platforms to transmit these corporate values on a permanent and continuous basis. This can be through "welcome plans" for new in-corporations that guarantee that professionals know the organization's values from the start, producing "situational training videos" on each corporate value where the desired

attitudes are exemplified, information pills such as rapid-learning, or more playful alternatives such as gamification that help to internalize them.

5. Although time and effort are spent on transmitting values, individuals (employees) will turn a deaf ear to anything that does not conform to the values they already have in their inner selves. Changing people's values is difficult and, to be realistic, almost impossible to do so when a certain maturity is reached. Assuming this premise, perhaps the best way to successfully transmit corporate values is to ensure that selection processes choose people whose values are compatible with those of the organization. You can also incentivize your employees to bring in like-minded referrals to join the team.
6. Ask for and provide feedback. In terms of feedback, it is a give-and-take process. Before the training, ask your employees what they would find most valuable to walk away with from this experience and how it can improve their work life and performance. Vice versa, providing your employees with feedback regarding their participation and implementation of the training helps you establish true value during and after the training process.
7. Whether you are training your employees through online courses and presentations or printed reading materials, everything needs to echo your company's mission and identity. Your employees will often be a customer's first point

of contact in the buying process. The way you speak and act toward your employees is likely how they are going to speak and act toward your customers. Always show them appreciation and respect. If your employees don't understand your brand identity, then they can't give customers the desired brand experience. Having brand-compliant training not only means using your brand elements, such as the company logo and brand colors on all of the materials, but also using the same tone and voice with your employees that you use with your customers. The way you train your employees should follow your company's values and beliefs.

8. It may seem obvious, but in order to successfully transmit corporate values, it is necessary to make them public in all possible ways: directly (through the usual internal communication channels) and indirectly (to which we must pay special attention). Values are conveyed by words, but above all, by deeds. It is important to act in accordance with these values on a daily basis and to work to imprint them in the processes of developing and executing the products and services delivered to customers.
9. Reward effort. When employees realize the results of their actions, it is much easier to engage them. Conduct and share regular status reviews with them, and make sure that their bonuses or variables are directly related to the value they bring to the brand. In addition to tangible rewards, there could be

intangible rewards such as awards for the best brand ambassadors.

To ensure success in communicating corporate values, follow each of the above points to reach people internally and externally. If you put each of the steps into practice continuously, you will never go wrong.

Core values exist in every workplace. Your organization's culture is partially the outward demonstration of the values currently existing in your workplace. The question you need to ask is whether these existing values are creating the workplace you desire. By implementing these values into every aspect of your business, including training, you're making sure the development of your employees and your company are in line with the true mission of your organization.

Let us not forget that one of the fundamental principles in building a brand is authenticity. That is why an employee cannot be forced to feel emotionally linked to the company and the brand that represents it. As with customers, it is necessary to build a two-way relationship and generate a brand experience also within the companies. This is the only way to ensure that the outward experience will reach its full potential.

In this chapter we have discussed the basic principles of building your brand image and the importance of harmonizing all the elements that constitute our corporate identity in order to connect with both audience and employees in a unique and honest way. Our identity, history, values, vision, and missions are the score under which we will begin to compose a symphony that resonates equally in each and every department of our company. These principles will be the fundamental pillars that will allow us to harmonize each and every one of the messages and actions that we carry out from now on.

Now that you have the basics to build your identity, let's see how to start implementing this new identity and harmonize it with the marketing, sales, and advertising departments.

CHAPTER 1 WORKSHEET

BRAND IDENTITY

It's time to put into practice what you learned in the first chapter, and for that, we bring to this worksheet the key questions to start building your brand identity and try to understand all aspects related to the feelings you convey to your customers and your employees. Take these exercises as a self-reflection and allow yourself to develop your ideas as much as you want until you come up with a cohesive identity that you are ready to work with. Let's get started.

WHAT FIVE WORDS DESCRIBE YOU?

Draw up a list of the five adjectives that most describe your brand personality.

1. ....
2. ....
3. ....
4. ....
5. ....

What are the specific qualities of the services and/or products you offer?

....

....

....

....

....

....

....

....

....

What are the core values of your products and services?

....

....

....

....

....

....

....

....

....

What does your company specialize in? That is, what is your niche?

……………………………………………………………………

……………………………………………………………………

……………………………………………………………………

……………………………………………………………………

……………………………………………………………………

……………………………………………………………………

……………………………………………………………………

……………………………………………………………………

……………………………………………………………………

Who is your target audience?

……………………………………………………………………

……………………………………………………………………

……………………………………………………………………

……………………………………………………………………

……………………………………………………………………

……………………………………………………………………

……………………………………………………………………

……………………………………………………………………

……………………………………………………………………

What is your company's slogan, and what kind of message does your slogan send to your potential customers? (If you don't have one, try to come up with a snappy one based on the first thing that pops into your head. The purpose is to summarize your value proposition in a concise and clear sentence that will catch the attention of your audience.)

It's time to create a personality for your company that clearly represents your products or services. Taking as a reference the twelve archetypes we have seen in the chapter, try to understand which of them best identifies with your brand, and explain why you think it is the best option. Describe the personality by choosing words you would use when writing your biography or explaining to a colleague why your business is unique. Be creative.

....

....

....

....

....

....

....

....

....

....

....

....

....

....

....

....

Now that you have described and internalized your brand personality, the next step will be a piece of cake. It's time to establish your company's mission and vision. To do this, try to answer the following questions with everything described previously in mind.

MISSION:

1. What do you want to offer?

....

....

....

....

....

....

....

....

....

2. Why did you want to create this business?

....

....

....

....

....

……………………………………………………………………

……………………………………………………………………

……………………………………………………………………

……………………………………………………………………

3. What is the user profile you want to attract?

……………………………………………………………………

……………………………………………………………………

……………………………………………………………………

……………………………………………………………………

……………………………………………………………………

……………………………………………………………………

……………………………………………………………………

……………………………………………………………………

……………………………………………………………………

4. What business image do you want to communicate?

……………………………………………………………………

……………………………………………………………………

……………………………………………………………………

……………………………………………………………………

……………………………………………………………………

....

....

....

....

5. What factors determine the price and quality of your products and/or services?

....

....

....

....

....

....

....

....

....

6. What relationship will you have with your employees?

....

....

....

....

………………………………………………………………………

………………………………………………………………………

………………………………………………………………………

………………………………………………………………………

………………………………………………………………………

7. What is your differentiating aspect that makes you stand out from your competitors?

………………………………………………………………………

………………………………………………………………………

………………………………………………………………………

………………………………………………………………………

………………………………………………………………………

………………………………………………………………………

………………………………………………………………………

………………………………………………………………………

………………………………………………………………………

VISION:

1. What will your company look like in a few years?

………………………………………………………………………

………………………………………………………………………

………………………………………………………………………

2. What are your short-, medium-, and long-term goals?

3. What will be the key values and attitudes of the company?

....

....

....

....

....

....

4. What do you want people to think of your company in the future?

....

....

....

....

....

....

....

....

....

5. What aspects of growth would you like to achieve?

....

....

....

....

....

....

....

....

VALUES:

We have listed a few companies and their values—like Google, Netflix, and Coca-Cola. Of those we have already mentioned, which of them most identify your company? If none, how are you different?

....

....

....

....

....

....

....

....

....

....

....

BRAND STORY:
Now, time to get inspired and write:

- How your story began.
- What was that peak moment when you felt the need to bring to life that project you had so much in mind?
- What difficulties you had (if any) in that initial stage.
- What was the "why" and how did you find the "why" and the "how"?
- What things have changed since you started your project?
- How you see yourself in a few years.
- What anecdotes or memories that come to mind?

....

....

....

....

....

....

....

....

....

....

....

Now let's write about a **success story with one of your customers**. Include the following:

- How did you meet them?
- What was their situation?
- What was their process?
- What were their struggles to achieve their goal?
- What were their initial fears?
- What were the things that made them believe in your brand?
- What is their life like today?

....

....

....

....

....

....

....

....

....

....

....

....

....

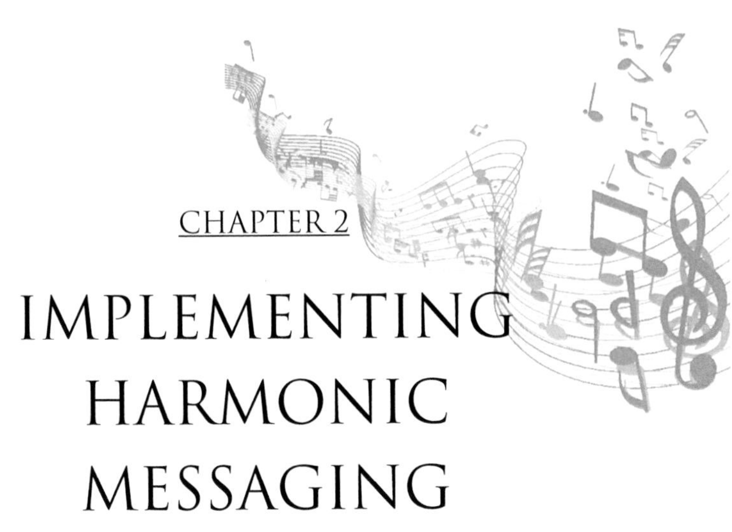

CHAPTER 2

IMPLEMENTING HARMONIC MESSAGING

Unity is strength . . . when there is teamwork and collaboration, wonderful things can be achieved.

—Mattie Stepanek

There are lots of advertising and marketing mediums right now, and marketing campaigns are becoming more powerful and creative. To stand out from the lot, you need to assert your presence through a consistent message and aggressive branding—not separately, but together.

We have delved into how we can create a strong brand identity and have learned how to transmit these values to the internal part of the company. It is time to start implementing our Harmonic Messaging externally. In this chapter we will explore and try to define how to take our new identity and make it permeate and work harmoniously in all areas of our company's branding, marketing, advertising, and sales.

I see a successful marketing campaign as a finely tuned system, with multiple parts working in harmony to achieve a single result. Your company should be like an orchestra: the sales department would be the winds, marketing the percussion, human resources the piano, operations the bass, and so on. No longer can you rely on just one thing to carry your brand. For example, in the past, you could rely on your company's excellent PR and history to attract customers. The entire orchestra must function in complete harmony, and that is only possible with powerful conducting.

Now, with so much competition and so many platforms to market on, someone is going to sweep the rug from under your feet if you're not careful. You can't settle for a shoddy and weak plan; brand communication must be strong and unified. It should be the core of all our songs.

Getting people to change the way they think about you is no easy task. You have to **deliver precisely targeted messages** that rise above the clutter and force them to change their assumptions.

Imagine attending an orchestra recital. The melodious symphony comes from the collective resonance of all the instruments. Each instrument has a specific task; the aim is for them to come together in a way that produces beautiful music. Integrated, or harmonic, brand communication is similar—here, advertising could be your violin, social media your piano, public relations your trumpet, and so on.

Harmonic brand communication is thus defined as the *process of organizing, planning, and monitoring brand components and data to control and influence brand information, associations, and experience.*

It involves the coordination and integration of all tools and departments into a single program that enhances the effect on end users and customers at minimum cost.

When a product is promoted effectively, brand awareness increases among the public. When people are more aware of your product, there are understandably more potential customers.

And, well, the rest follows: more sales, revenue, and profit figures.

To this end, organizations strive to increase the popularity of products among potential end users. Brand communication is the process adopted by companies to make their products more popular and attractive to end users.

Brand communication promotes products through many possible means, such as:

- *traditional and digital advertising,*
- *sales promotions,*
- *personal selling,*
- *direct marketing,*
- *public relations,*
- *social media,*
- *and many more.*

By collaborating across departments, organizations ensure that their messages and promotions are consistent and unified. Harmonious communication combines all the tools, resources, and approaches available to an organization to create an impact and a footprint in the minds of consumers. This results in high amounts of benefits at relatively low costs—you would not need to advertise every time because your brand is already in the consumer's mind.

Innovation is the cornerstone of all integrated communication; companies must employ creative ways to ensure that customers receive the right message in the right place at the right time.

Conceptually, it is a simple technique. An organization links all promotional tools so that they work in harmony and deliver a consistent message. However, its implementation is an entirely different task and requires careful planning and coordination between the teams involved.

Why Is It Effective to Harmonize Your Campaigns?

While communications campaigns may differ in their objectives (e.g., converting visitors, building brand awareness, etc.), they should all have one component in common: aligning your marketing channels to present a unified marketing "front."

If your marketing channels are players, consider your harmonic marketing campaign to be the coach in charge of directing the plays and helping your channels function as a unified—not disparate—system. In a nutshell, as a team.

It's also more effective to run harmonic campaigns compared to different campaigns on individual channels. Harmonic campaigns are impactful for several reasons:

- They reach a broader audience than a single marketing channel.
- They have a higher likelihood of being seen on multiple channels, thus keeping your brand top-of-mind and pushing visitors closer to conversion.
- They build trust with visitors, as they see a consistent message across multiple channels.

- They save you money, as assets can be shared and reused for different marketing channels, and, depending on your campaign, customers can help you market your product or service.

Defining Your Brand's Communicational Tone

People can be very sensitive to language and tend to create impressions of brands as soon as they start reading their copy. That's why brand tone should be distinctive, recognizable, and unique.

A brand's tone of voice is not what you say, but how you say it. This encompasses not only the words you choose but also their order, form, and rhythm. In the business world and in marketing strategies, it refers to written words rather than spoken words. A brand should use friendly language to make its writing familiar to the customer (i.e., create a specific tone of voice). Words should be chosen carefully and can be used to persuade or influence an audience. In general, a successful brand tone should go unannounced.

Brand tone represents the personality and values of your brand and applies to all the content you deliver. From website content, social media posts, emails, and any other format. Properly defined and implemented tone of voice allows your brand to be recognized by your audience just by reading it, even if they don't see your logo or company name attached to the content it produces.

To define our brand tone we must take into account everything we learned in the previous chapter about our brand identity. What is your brand like? What are its values? What audience are you targeting? How do your potential customers communicate with each other? With the answers to all these questions in mind, you should know what tone you should use to best connect with your audience.

With these elements defined, clear guidelines can be established to ensure that your brand tone is reflected in all communications your brand sends out and in all your marketing strategies. As team members become familiar with the guidelines and how to use the brand's preferred tone, it becomes easier to create new content that aligns with this vision.

Before creating a brand tone that fits your company, audit your existing content and communications to see what your brand sounds like right now. To do this, make a list of your best performing (according to your content metrics) and best (in your opinion) assets, and ask yourself if your current brand tone:

- Does it match the brand values you want to communicate?
- Does it reflect your values as described in your mission statement to your audience?
- Does it match your message architecture?

Review each piece of content and record (e.g., in a spreadsheet) what your brand sounds like. To help content strategists and other specialists analyze a website's brand tone, *Nielsen Norman Group*[1] identified four dimensions of tone of voice:

1. *Fun vs. serious*

---

[1] "The Four Dimensions of Tone of Voice," https://www.nngroup.com/articles/tone-of-voice-dimensions/.

2. *Formal vs. casual*
3. *Respectful vs. irreverent*
4. *Enthusiastic vs. natural*

Implement changes in your business communication. To successfully implement your brand tone, start by establishing clear brand guidelines and make sure they are reviewed from time to time, especially when there are changes in your positioning and target audience.

Clear guidelines, rules, and positive examples give people the confidence to write in this new way. Many brands have them, but only a few have formal guidelines that are consistently applied.

Your internal guidelines should include:

- a portrait of your target audience and their voice;
- your brand's attitude toward its audience (a best friend, an aunt, a teacher . . .);
- your brand's core values;
- mission statement;
- message architecture;
- brand voice charter;
- specific vocabulary and grammatical rules;
- clear examples in different contexts;
- introduce rules for your brand's tone of use.

Assign responsibility for enforcing the guidelines to a team member, such as an editor or content manager. This will help ensure that all your brand communications use the right words to distribute the right tone across all content.

Your brand tone should be unique to your business. It should be tailored to the brand, needs, message, and the expectations of your customers. **Create a tone style guide**, be consistent across all channels, look at how your competition behaves, how they carry the message, and reflect yourself in that mirror. Share all this information with the different departments of your company so that all communications resonate at the same tempo.

It will take some time to perfect your brand tone, but implementing it into your marketing strategies will help you take the first steps toward building that recognizable brand identity.

HOW TO BUILD A HARMONIC MESSAGING CAMPAIGN

Now that we have understood the importance of uniting all our communication strategies around our new identity in order to achieve our objectives, and we have established the right tone for our communicational campaign, you may ask yourself, *How can I start designing my strategy in a harmonious and integrated way?* Let's take a look:

1. **Establish the overall objective of your campaign.**

Before considering which channels will be part of your campaign, you should consider the goal of the entire campaign.

Perhaps you have launched a new product, service, or initiative and want to get the word out to customers. Perhaps you have completely rebranded and want to get your new message out. Maybe you've simply chosen a new positioning tagline and want your audience to start associating your brand with it, like Snickers' "You're Not You When You're Hungry."

Whatever your campaign goal is, always remember to keep it SMART. This will help you stay focused, track the success of your campaign, and learn how to improve next time.

SMART objectives are specific goals that are intended to be achieved during a given period. These objectives must be carefully drafted by a manager and his or her direct subordinate to be successful. "SMART" is an acronym that describes the most important characteristics of each objective.

The acronym "SMART" stands for "specific," "measurable," "achievable," "relevant," and "time-bound." Each SMART objective must have these five characteristics to ensure that the objective is achievable and benefits the employee.

Let's see an example of what a SMART goal looks like:

Brand affinity objective

Specific: I want to increase the number of listeners to our podcast, as we are trying to establish ourselves as thought leaders in our market.

Measurable: Our goal is to increase the number of listeners by 40 percent.

Achievable: We can increase our current budget and level the cadence of our podcasters so that we have the means to have insightful conversations for our listeners to tune in.

Relevant: We've created a podcast and dedicated a team to finding interesting guests, sound mixing, and eye-catching thumbnails to get it off the ground.

Time-bound: In four months.

SMART Goal: In four months, we'll see a 40 percent increase in the average number of listeners on Apple

Podcasts by providing our team with the budget and cadence to make interesting podcasts with a quality sound mix and eye-catching thumbnails.

These goals should also relate to at least one of the key performance indicators (KPIs) and their subsequent metrics, which you can track when you launch your campaign.

In addition, while increased engagement and new leads are always exciting, a multichannel campaign should also take into account the big picture: how the campaign affects the company's sales opportunities and revenue. Take a moment to plan how you want your campaign to impact your profit and loss statement as well.

2. **Choose your marketing channels and set objectives for each of them.**

Now that you know the overall objective of your marketing campaign, you probably have a better idea of which (if not all) channels can help you achieve that objective.

For example, if your goal is to launch a new logo and set of brands, you don't necessarily need to leverage radio ads. On the other hand, if you are expanding your audience to target a new geographic region or city, radio ads, billboards, TV spots, and other local channels may be useful.

When it comes to choosing your channel(s), it all comes down to what you are trying to achieve with your campaign. There are ten major marketing "channels" you can use to distribute your campaign content.

1. *Advertising (both print and PPC)*
2. *Direct marketing*

3. *Email marketing*
4. *Public relations*
5. *Personal selling*
6. *Sales promotions*
7. *Digital marketing (e.g., website, content marketing, and SEO)*
8. *Social media*
9. *Events and sponsorships*
10. *Packaging*

Your harmonious campaign should include a variety of marketing channels to reach the most people and deliver your campaign message. If you see one or more channels becoming stagnant, don't hesitate to add, remove, or try new ones.

3. Define your buyer personas by channel.

A buyer persona is a semi-fictional profile of the ideal customer of your brand or company; it represents the people you want to attract, convert, and delight with your product or service in order to make a sale.

Each channel targets its own specific buyer persona. For this reason, rather than defining a broad persona for your campaign, you should define your audience by channel.

Inevitably, there will be some overlap, but it pays to understand exactly who you are targeting in each medium and how you can tailor those specific assets to be most successful.

In some campaigns, you may target a specific audience. In this case, steps 2 and 3 would be reversed: you would first define your buyer(s) and then decide which channels can help you reach that audience.

4. **Identify your channel managers.**

Depending on the size of your marketing team, you may have different people (or entire teams) in charge of different channels. When running a multichannel marketing campaign, you need to determine who specifically will be in charge of ensuring that your channel(s) are aligned with the campaign.

This is important for two reasons: (1) that person in charge is the expert on your channel (e.g., audience, posting cadence, optimization tactics, reporting strategies, etc.) and will know how to tailor the campaign content to be as successful as possible; and (2) putting one person in charge of all channels can be overwhelming and will cause the content and campaign to suffer.

Perhaps you have a smaller marketing team where one person is in charge of multiple channels. Regardless of the size of your team, do your best to share channel management responsibilities among a few people, ideally with one person handling one or two channels

5. **Create adaptable marketing assets and messages.**

At this point, you have your campaign objective, target audience, and marketing channels. Now it's time to create the content for your harmonic marketing campaign. Copywriting, graphic design, and other creative processes come into play at this stage.

Before we get into the how, let's talk about an important component of harmonic marketing content: adaptability. To keep your campaign consistent (and ease your workload), you need to be able to repurpose any content for use across different channels.

For example, let's say your campaign centers around the launch of a new three-minute branded video. You could repurpose this video into:

- Thirty-second and one-minute "trailer" videos
- Still images
- Quotes
- GIFs
- Hashtags
- Blog posts
- Soundbites

As you develop and repurpose these creative assets, keep them aligned with your brand guidelines and consistent with each other. In fact, it may be helpful to create your own set of brand guidelines for your Harmonic Messaging campaign to share with your team and any channel managers.

This documentation could include a few things:

- Visual guidelines (logo, color palette, typography, etc.)
- Any assets developed and reused in multiple file formats
- Voice and tone guidelines (taglines, preferred language, words to avoid, etc.)
- Message guidelines (pain points, objectives, content types, assets, etc.)
- Buyer information and guidelines

Harmonic Messaging relies on a consistent brand experience. Make sure your campaign assets reflect this, regardless of the channel your audience visits or views.

6. Establish your lead-nurturing plan.

Whether or not the intent of your campaign is to collect leads, you should always be prepared to receive them. You don't want to leave this as an afterthought once you've launched your campaign. Even if you're simply running a campaign to raise awareness of your brand, consider how your visitors might convert into leads and, ultimately, customers.

First, **consider how a visitor might convert into a lead**. Would they subscribe to your newsletter? Would they enter their details to download a content offer? Would they create an account on your website? Make sure these conversion aspects of your campaign are in line with the rest of your visual and messaging assets.

Next, consider how your leads would be nurtured once they convert. Would they be included in an automated email workflow? Would you pass them on to sales? Whatever the case, make sure you don't forget about your leads once they've provided their information.

As always, contact sales to confirm that they are aware of your campaign and are on board with your plan for new leads and customers.

7. Launch, measure, and repeat your campaign.

Are you ready to launch your integrated marketing campaign? It may be time to launch your campaign . . . but it's not time to rest yet.

Remember the KPIs and metrics? Whatever KPIs relate to the overall goal of your campaign (e.g., increase brand awareness, rebrand, create a new product, etc.), start tracking those subsequent metrics every week, every month, and every quarter (depending on how long your campaign lasts) to see how successful you are in achieving your goal.

As always, take what you learn from each campaign and apply it to future campaigns. With the right strategies, managers, and tools, you can create an endless cycle of Harmonic Messaging campaigns—and wins.

HARMONIC MESSAGING STRATEGIES AND BEST PRACTICES

When building your HM campaign, there are some key strategies and best practices to keep in mind. We've detailed them here, and they apply regardless of the media, channels, or objectives you've chosen.

Align Behind the Scenes

To successfully implement a harmonious marketing approach, it is imperative not only to choose the marketing channel managers but also that all managers communicate often about projects and campaigns.

While not all campaigns or promotions need to be on all your channels, they should at least complement each other to avoid a fragmented brand experience for customers. It is also important to keep all employees involved informed so that they are aware of the message you want to convey correctly and consistently.

Be Mindful of Channel Transition

Integrated campaigns receive traffic from multiple

sources and pass them along like a game of hot potato. Consider how a visitor might view/experience each marketing channel (1) if it's their first visit, and (2) if they transition from another channel. Think about how each channel can help others convert.

For example, let's say a customer saw your new billboard on their way to work and, once they arrived, they visited the website featured on the billboard. Imagine if, on your website, the customer couldn't easily find what your billboard was marketing. Would that be too confusing? That customer would probably abandon immediately.

Don't Neglect Small Overlaps

When preparing to launch your campaign, it's tempting to think separately about each channel and their respective media. But this thought process inherently goes against the spirit of HM. This strategy exists to eradicate traditional marketing silos and bring together a cohesive campaign experience.

For this reason, don't neglect the places where your campaign overlaps. Here are a few examples:

- Your email signature, where you can include the names of your social networks, your website URL, or video links. If you have a newsletter, make sure all elements are cohesive with all elements of your identity.
- Your bios and social media posts, where you can include links to your website, blog posts, content offerings, or other digital content. Post consistently and engage with potential partners and customers.
- Your blog and website, where you can

incorporate social sharing buttons. Post shareable content on social media and keep your visitors engaged by posting call-to-action words that drive conversation.

- Your standalone landing pages, where you can optimize for relevant keywords and SEO.
- Your SEO. You should aim to be optimized to rank on the first page of Google. You can achieve this by writing blog posts, making videos, and getting links to other websites related to your industry.
- Your PPC copy, where you can test subject lines to see what your audience responds to. You could run ads that offer introductory content or solve a pain point.
- Your videos, where you can take advantage of pulling testimonials, behind-the-scenes footage, and even videos of your employees explaining what their day-to-day life is like at the company. This immediately connects with your audience and reinforces your identity if you apply consistency in your messaging.
- Your PR team can take your identity to another level to connect with different audiences through events, sponsorships, volunteering, or media interventions such as radio or TV.
- Your referral partners must also be on the same page as your brand identity, so it is essential to ensure that they maintain the coherence, tone, and image of your brand so that the message effectively reaches your potential customers.

While these overlaps may not directly support your campaign objectives, they help your audience move seamlessly from channel to channel, enjoy a consistent and cohesive brand experience, and ultimately find their way to a page that converts for them.

CASE STUDIES

SNICKERS

You have probably heard of "You're not you when you're hungry." The famous Snickers tagline implies that the chocolate bar is a great on-the-go snack, and relieves you of hunger.

Snickers continued this program through print, digital, display, and television media, and even at the retail level. Consistent messaging and branding resulted in this easily distinguishable sentence that, when you hear it, you immediately think of Snickers.

GOPRO

The GoPro utilized components of harmonious messaging to great effect. They used their geared campaigns to appeal to the masses. GoPro has mastered online content to catch the attention of an audience. Their YouTube channel displays videos shot using their action camera taken by the company itself and its users.

Their social media following is also significant, and they use these platforms to post more visually appealing videos taken with the action cameras. GoPro also conducts online contests almost every day with chances to win prizes. This form of event also acts as publicity, and the number of entrants every day shows how effective it is.

The company's "Be A Hero" campaign spanned many platforms, such as print, display, and online. The program was created to market their "Hero" product line and centered on the idea that "anyone who pursues their passion and lives life to the fullest is a hero."

This spawned many video clips and shots by these heroes, such as the adventurous divers and ambitious surfers. Through a singular brand message—"Everyone is a hero, and they are all around us"—GoPro appealed to emotion and passion.

ALWAYS

Always, as a feminine care brand, is advocating itself as a voice for good. Many studies outline that a girl's confidence and self-esteem lower as they reach the puberty stage.

Always came up with their #LikeAGirl campaign to combat this self-esteem crisis. The program aims to change the way people perceive the phrase "You ____ like a girl."

The company pushed the campaign to multiple mediums such as social media, television, and print.

The campaign's video was considered more of a documentary on the perception of girls about themselves and won multiple awards from the British charity, Design and Art Direction. With more than 65 million YouTube views, the campaign is considered a success; the video still receives new comments every day.

EMIRATES

Emirates started with two leased aircraft in 1985 and hasn't looked back since. Today, the airline operates 265 aircraft to more than 155 destinations.

Emirates' harmonic marketing communications approach:

- *Traditional media*: Emirates' advertising and print ads in major media highlight the airline's new products, flight routes, and aircraft.
- *Event sponsorship*: The airline actively sponsors a host of sporting events such as soccer, horse racing, and tennis. It has also signed a sponsorship agreement with major soccer clubs such as Arsenal. Its presence in the Asian Football Confederation has also ensured it high visibility throughout Asia.
- *Own media*: The company publishes two in-flight magazines to reach out to its customers. A brilliant in-flight entertainment system allows the airline to publicize its latest offers, partners, and services. In addition, the company's official website allows customers to purchase branded products.
- *Appealing to millennials*: The airline is adopting a sustainable environmental strategy to protect natural resources and reduce air pollution. It is going one step ahead and ensuring that its fleet is updated with the most modern and fuel-efficient aircraft. Emirates uses various marketing communication tools in an integrated way to convey a unified message.
- *The high quality of its services*: Emirates presents the high quality of its air services as the underlying theme of all its marketing activities.

CHAPTER 2 WORKSHEET

DEFINING BRAND'S TONE OF VOICE

In defining your pitch, you will want a format that is

easy for everyone to understand, and ideally quantifiable in some way. This way, you can have constructive discussions where you can explain why something "doesn't sound right" and make meaningful improvements.

To address all of these needs, we have created two simple exercises to help you define your brand's tone of voice. For these exercises to be effective, of course, you'll need to think about what kind of tone is aligned with your customers' needs. Take everything you learned in the previous chapter and in the exercises already completed as a reference.

The material in the exercises has been adapted from research conducted by Nielsen Norman Group. They explain the approach of their research in the articles "The Four Dimensions of Tone of Voice" and "Tone of Voice Words."

Let's start with a simple one. Sometimes, to know what you are, it also helps to know what you are not. Try to fill in the blanks in this sentence:

We're _______, but we're not _______ .

Then, repeat this process several times until you arrive at three or four sentences that best describe your brand. Here's what this might look like when you're finished:

> "We're authoritative, but not too serious."
> "We're funny, but not sarcastic."
> "We're friendly, but not sappy."

....

....

....

....

....

....

....

Create a Brand Voice Chart

Next, take the three or four words that best represent your brand, explaining how each feature should and should not be represented in your marketing:

1. List your brand characteristics on the left.
2. Include a brief explanation of each trait in the next column.
3. Explain how to use (and not use) this trait in the next two columns.

TRAIT	DESCRIPTION	DO	DON'T

Keep this on hand for writers to use as a reference.

Now that we know who we are, who our audience is, and how we communicate with them, we are ready to **launch our harmonic campaign**. Let's start by establishing our objectives. As we have seen, these should be SMART.

INITIAL GOAL	**Write the goal you have in mind.**
SPECIFIC	**What do you want to accomplish? Who needs to be included? Why is this a goal?**
MEASURABLE	**How can you measure progress and know if you've successfully met your goal?**
ACHIEVABLE	**Do you have the skills required to achieve the goal? If not, can you obtain them? What is the motivation for this goal? Is the amount of effort required on par with what the goal will achieve?**
RELEVANT	**Why am I setting this goal now? Is it aligned with overall objectives?**
TIME-BOUND	**What's the deadline? Is it realistic?**
SMART GOAL	**Review what you have written and craft a new goal statement based on what the answers to the questions above have revealed.**

Now it's time to select our channels and define the buyer personas for each of those channels.

To find our **buyer persona**, we must have researched our audience in depth and know which channels each of them uses. For example, let's say you have a bike store. Your buyer persona might be someone in their twenties who spends their time on Instagram, but at the same time you might also want to target people in their forties who might prefer to use Facebook. You need to know your audience and know where they connect, how they talk, how they interact with others, and what their needs and pain points are. Below there is an example. Use the template to create a buyer persona and replicate this same technique for all the channels and audience types you want to reach.

CHAPTER 3

HARMONIC CUSTOMER JOURNEY

Get closer than ever to your customers. So close that you tell them what they need well before they realize it themselves.

—Steve Jobs

Now that we have seen how to harmonize our communication campaign, it is time to put it into practice and delve deeper into the customer journey from the moment they learn about our brand until they buy one of our products. Maintaining consistency and coherence in our harmonic strategy at all times will be key to our company's success. Let's look at the customer journey and how we can harmonize the process to improve our reputation and brand awareness.

THE AIDA MODEL

The AIDA model has been used by advertisers and marketers for several decades: due to its high effectiveness, its application has spread to practically all areas of marketing. Today, it is a copywriting method widely used in content marketing, as it allows to capture the user's attention, add value, and, therefore, increase the number of visits to a company's website.

This technique works based on the different phases of the sales funnel and, like it, it is structured in four stages. Find out below what the AIDA method is and how you can add it to your copy to attract prospects and increase your sales.

What Does AIDA Mean?

The AIDA concept is an acronym formed by the terms "attention," "interest," "desire," and "action." It is based on the process that a user goes through from the moment he/she discovers a brand, becomes interested in what it offers, desires it, purchases it, and becomes a customer.

It is one of the first persuasive copywriting formulas created to lead people to perform a specific action—in this case, a purchase.

The main objective of the AIDA method is to make a sale. During the process, for each of the phases of the process, different strategies are applied to allow the prospect to advance to the next stage.

> *The AIDA method was created by Elmo Lewis, a pioneer in sales and advertising in the United States, in 1899.*

Here, you will learn about the different stages and the strategies you can use in each one of them.

ATTENTION

This is the first stage of the buying process. During this stage, users become aware that they have a need or desire to fulfill. The AIDA method seeks to attract their attention to bring them closer to what they need.

As in any marketing strategy, it is necessary to know your target audience in depth. You must be clear about their interests, motivations, and main characteristics in order to achieve a detailed segmentation. This will allow you to send well-personalized content and messages that are effective in attracting users.

In addition to knowing your audience, you must be very clear about your value proposition. What differentiates you from your competitors? What can you offer that they are not able to provide?

The first thing readers notice while browsing is the headline—this is the first contact users have with your content and it is essential to write with persuasive headline techniques.

Here are some examples of structures you can use to create impactful and attractive titles:

How to + verb + noun + benefit.
Example: "How to Transform Leads into Customers in an Automated Way"
Number + Noun + Verb + Compliment
Example: "7 Out of 10 Families Enjoy On-Demand Platforms for Entertainment"
Verb/Desire + Compliment/Negation
Example: "Enjoy a Balanced Figure without Going Hungry"
Get + Desire + in + Desired Tense
Example: "Get Your Hair Looking Healthy and Shiny in Just Two Weeks"

The rule of three: word/phrase + word/phrase + word/phrase + word/phrase
Example: "Homemade Face Masks for Healthy Skin. Healthy Eating."

In these formulas, some of the most effective techniques in copywriting are represented. The questions that include the readers make them feel involved and generate interest. Also, numbers—mainly odd numbers—have proven to have a high attraction potential. Action verbs such as "discover," "learn," "achieve," "transform," etc. are highly effective.

On the other hand, touching on your customers' pain points (which refer to problems they need to solve) is an excellent technique to motivate them to read your content. Make them find with you what they were looking for.

INTEREST

Interest is the second stage that people go through in the buying process. At this stage, users already recognize their needs and begin to investigate products and services that can meet them.

You have managed to attract the user and the time comes when you must keep their attention so that they continue to learn about your brand and your products. At this point, content becomes a little more personalized.

You no longer need to talk about problems in general, but you can educate users about the different ways to solve a certain problem and explain how to do it. The close tone and the formulation of direct questions in the titles are still effective resources for this stage.

Seek to empathize with your users and appeal to their emotions to keep their interest.

Desire

At this stage, users are already informed about the possible solutions to their problem, need, or desire, and begin to investigate the different options available in the market to make up their minds.

Nowadays, people have thousands of alternatives just a click away; therefore, you must work on creating excellent content to stand out from your competitors. This is the moment when you must demonstrate why your product is the best option.

Work on the transformative effects of your products. Show how, through your goods or services, users will move from situation A (the need) to situation B (the dream).

To work on this "transformation," you should emphasize the benefits of your product, which are neither physical nor technical features—refer to the longed-for change that someone can achieve thanks to your brand.

Another effective technique is to point out the possible consequences of not solving a problem in time. This is a way that appeals to the customers' pain points and generates great results.

These are two different methodologies, but equally efficient. You can evaluate them and decide which one best suits the spirit and essence of your company.

Action

The final stage has to do with action and occurs when users have already decided to make a purchase. The content generated should be focused on making this moment as simple as possible and, to finish convincing them, you can motivate customers with a discount or promotion.

If everything has gone well, users will take action—that

is, they will actually make the purchase. Here, it is crucial to make things easy for them.

In addition, in this instance you can offer them advantages for making their purchase at that moment. To complete the process, you need to add an attractive call to action (CTA). The ideal is to use direct and actionable verbs.

To make these calls to action even more irresistible, you can use the following tips:

Add exclusive bonuses: *"Buy now and get a free gift."*
Use urgency and scarcity: *"Limited offer," "last day," "only 10 places."*

Remember the beneficial conditions. Guarantees, free shipping, free trial periods, etc.

To conclude, there are two types of effective CTAs:

Speaking in the first person: *"I want to book my spot."*
Speaking in the second person: *"Book your spot now."*

In the first case, the aim is to make the customer feel identified and internalize the action to be taken; in the second case, we ask them to take action by directly questioning them.

This is a **case study** from one of our clients showing how a well-known hairdressing company used the model to launch their new salon.

1. **Awareness**: A PR campaign was conducted four months prior to launch, promoting the

award, stylists, qualifications, etc., and reinforced by a DM campaign targeting specific customer groups.

2. **Interest**: A direct mail campaign was conducted to offer a free consultation or haircut and finish. They used research to support that this would work, as women are loyal if the offer is compelling.
3. **Desire**: Near the opening of the new salon, they organized exclusive local launch events that were advertised in the local press and on social media. This created a buzz among people who wanted an invitation and were eager to see the new salon.
4. **Action**: Clear CTAs were positioned on the Facebook site (call to book), website (call to book), and local advertising (call to receive the discount or offer).

The case study did not highlight retention, although there are many ways to increase loyalty around signing up for mailing lists or social platforms that offer news about offers and events, discounts on product ranges, discounts based on frequency of visit, etc.

AIDA: TIPS TO GENERATE ATTRACTIVE COPYWRITING

If you want to apply the AIDA model to your content and take advantage of all its benefits, you will find useful tips here to generate attractive and persuasive copywriting.

Write for Your Buyer Persona

The key to successful copywriting is to create relevant

content for your buyer personas. To do this, you must know in depth what topics they are interested in, what their desires are, and what problems they have. In this way, you will be able to create more personal messages and arouse the interest of users.

You can, for example, use specific details that apply to your buyer personas, such as questions related to their tastes or consumer habits. It is also useful to refer to the latest trends in the digital world that everyone is talking about, such as the latest viral video on TikTok or the trending topic on Twitter.

Be Credible

Creating eye-catching and engaging headlines is crucial to being credible. However, it is very important that you also deliver what you promise. If you indicate in a headline that you are going to offer a certain type of content, it is essential that the article has the promised information.

If you only focus on creating attractive titles, but your content is poor and redundant, you will end up disappointing users who enter your website; most likely, they will not stay on it and will not come back.

Think of a Creative Title

As we mentioned before, headings are the first marketing and advertising element users see. If your headlines are not effective, they will decrease the chances of increasing your conversions and improving your sales.

To develop headlines with the AIDA model, you should focus on your buyer persona's problems and offer them specific solutions for the needs they have in their daily lives. For example, "*7 Techniques to Increase Your Leads in 2021.*" This type of title is very appealing, as it promises a list of tips aimed at marketers who need to increase their leads and conversions.

Use Style Elements

People react not only to what the ad says but also to how it looks. You can highlight ideas and reinforce the AIDA message by using underlining, bolding, italics, or hashtags.

Try to balance your content, as adding too much formatting can be overwhelming. Use these resources to guide users' reading and highlight the most important aspects.

Perform A/B Testing of Your Copywriting

An effective method to optimize your texts, both your emails and your blog, is to perform A/B tests. These tests consist of taking two identical emails and changing an element in one of them to test results with the same audience.

You can take just the headline of an email, modify it, and send it to your customers to see which option works best. This technique is applicable in subject lines, headlines, first paragraphs, images, or calls to action.

The more A/B testing you do, the more effective your content will be. Over time, you will be able to achieve the exact combination of elements that will allow you to increase the open rate and the number of clicks.

WHY APPLY AIDA IN YOUR HM STRATEGY?

In any purchase, both digital and face-to-face, the customer goes sequentially through the phases of attention, interest, desire, and action. What digital marketing has, unlike traditional marketing, is the ability to measure everything and perform optimization actions to improve results.

This possibility has allowed the AIDA model to adapt

to the new digital environment to attract users, convert visits into leads, close sales, and subsequently delight customers to be the best promoters of a brand.

One of the digital marketing strategies that resembles the AIDA model is Inbound Marketing. It focuses on the stages of the user's buying process and, through its content, seeks to attract, convert, sell, and delight customers.

Inbound Marketing and the AIDA model combine perfectly and are applicable for the same objectives. The main benefits of implementing the AIDA model in digital marketing are the following:

- Helps to organize. The AIDA model allows you to create an orderly and structured strategy to work stage by stage with specific objectives in each phase.
- Work with all the elements. This technique allows unifying all the elements of the market: company, product, and customer.
- It favors sales processes. AIDA is a methodology aimed at achieving effective and verifiable sales.
- Greater participation. The method can be applied in multiple multichannel strategies to attract users to your content.
- User activation. Not only can you use this model to increase your sales but also for any action you want users to take on your website (subscription, material download, etc.).
- Nurturing. In conjunction with automation tools, you can obtain information from your leads and, in this way, nurture them correctly to prepare them for the sale.

AIDA: SUCCESSFUL COPYWRITING CASES

Read on to learn about successful copywriting cases that use the AIDA method as a core strategy.

Neil Patel

Neil Patel is one of the most recognized experts in the digital marketing industry of this era. His own Facebook Ads demonstrate how to apply the AIDA method to perfection.

First, he works on attention with a question: "Do you want to learn how to increase traffic to your business and convert your visitors into actual PAYING customers?"

He then moves on to the interest stage, where he tells about well-known companies he has worked with (such as NBC or Amazon). After that, the desire is enhanced with the invitation to the FREE webinar (in capital letters).

And, finally, the call to action appears in a simple "sign up" button, thus completing the whole scheme.

Let's see the case of a big company:

Apple

As it is the largest company in the world (today), there are many things that they have surely done well. Let's take a look at how Apple used the AIDA model in its legendary iPhone introduction.

The first one, done by Steve Jobs.

Attention

Apple announced that they were about to introduce a new product—something no one had seen before.

Expectations and "Attention" were high.

Interest

Steve Jobs explained the technical characteristics of the product before showing it.

This made people focus more on the great features of the iPhone.

Desire

Once people knew what this product was capable of, Steve Jobs showed it.

He also highlighted some features that people had always Desired.

Action

Finally, Steve Jobs showed some Action: he used it.

Showing evidence that it was real and "reachable."

DOMINO'S

Domino's Pizza is an American fast food company that, due to its immense success, became a multinational company. For the growth of the brand, marketing was a key element.

Its value proposition has always been the speed of its delivery service. For this reason, their strategies when communicating with their customers revolve around this concept. In the following ad, we can find the elements of the AIDA model.

First, the attraction and interest is generated in the title: "How to get a pizza very fast (like, really fast)." Then, the desire is developed in the simple step-by-step to place the order. The action culminates with the promise to have the pizza in less than two minutes and, if not fulfilled, the reward is to get the next one for free.

When you work with a comprehensive strategy based

on your company's buyer personas, the AIDA formula is very effective. To achieve the task that this model proposes, you have to carefully craft headlines, body copy, and calls to action.

In short, it's all about generating content that is interesting to the people you want to reach.

Put this technique into practice and you'll quickly notice an improvement in the focus of your marketing efforts. For further optimization, A/B test each element until you find the perfect formula to get your prospects' attention, interest, and desire, and move them to action.

ENHANCE CUSTOMER JOURNEY WITH HYPER HARMONIC MESSAGING

Lack of knowledge of the customer decision-making process leads to missed opportunities and ineffective marketing. Knowing why, when, how, and where customers engage with your content is essential for brands that want to interact with customers when, how, and where it matters most. Crafting a data-driven customer decision journey is essential to help you create relevant harmonic brand messages to engage customers and get the desired response. In music and in leadership, timing is everything. And you can't have that kind of rhythm without listening.

We have entered an era where customers define how they engage with companies. With consumers in the driver's seat, traditional marketing strategies, processes, and tactics must change. Fortunately, when integrated marketing processes are properly incorporated, there can be a direct correlation between better marketing ROI and a better customer experience. Having the right technology and marketing automation in place can make a significant difference in the level of success of your marketing.

A well-designed customer journey is what creates good customer service and a sense of satisfaction at all stages of the sales funnel.[2] Improving the customer journey is one element of a successful marketing strategy because the more satisfied customers are with the buying process, the more likely they are to convert. In addition, you can also develop a stronger relationship with existing customers and quickly transform prospects into loyal customers by offering them the most comfortable customer journey possible. This clearly means more revenue too!

What Is the Customer Journey?

The customer journey refers to the total experiences customers have when they interact with your brand throughout the stages of the sales funnel. This journey includes when they become aware of your brand, become interested in your product, make the decision to buy from you instead of your competitor, and finally take the purchase action.

Knowing the details of the customer journey allows you to offer the best services to your potential customers so that they have valuable interactions with your brand. That feeling of happiness that accompanies a purchase is what you should focus on creating. When your customers are satisfied with their first purchase, they are more likely to come back for more.

---

[2] A sales funnel is a graphic representation of the sales stages a customer goes through when buying a product. This concept is based on the idea that all customers are led through more or less the same phases when making a purchase, the first step of the traditional sales funnel being the awareness stage, while the last one is the post-purchase evaluation. https://www.omniconvert.com/what-is/sales-funnel/.

Why You Need a Customer Journey Map

A customer journey map is a visual representation of the customer journey. It tells the story of the customers who interact with your brand from the moment they meet you to the moment they form a long-term relationship with you. Creating a customer journey map helps companies put themselves in their customers' shoes and see their business from the customers' perspective. It also allows marketers to uncover their customers' pain points and learn how to overcome buying obstacles. To maximize the benefits of this map, it is advisable to make different maps for each of the buyer persona types we have recognized.

Customers want brands to understand their needs. They expect companies to make the information they need available to them without having to complain to find the answer. This is where a customer journey map helps—it reveals potential problems the customer may have when considering the purchase of how and how those problems can be solved.

Other advantages of a customer journey map are as follows:

- Allows you to focus on the customer's specific needs at each stage of the journey.
- Allows you to determine how to create content and personalize it.
- It gives you the customer's perspective on your sales process so you can empathize with them.
- Allows you to focus your efforts on the stages that matter most to ensure a better customer experience.
- Answers potential questions up front.

- Reduces buying obstacles by resolving pain points.
- . . . and much more.

An Example of a Customer Journey

Your customer is walking through downtown and sees your store window and the sign indicating that you sell women's shoes. She walks in and looks at the layout of the store. Your assistant greets her and offers to help her find what she is looking for. Your assistant is friendly and knowledgeable. She provides you with information about all the shoes the customer is interested in and helps her choose the pair of shoes that fits her needs.

The assistant assures the customer that if she is not satisfied with the pair of shoes, she can return them no questions asked. She then collects her email address to inform her of new arrivals. Later, the customer posts a photo of her new shoes and tags the store. She then logs on to yelp.com and recommends your services. She is clearly impressed by your brand.

In this customer journey example, you can see that the customer is happy throughout her interactions with the shoe brand. She loves how you helped her make the right decision based on her needs and assured her of a refund if she wasn't satisfied with the pair of shoes. Because of her excellent experience, she posts her shoes on social media and associates with your brand. Her friends will be interested in buying the same shoes or they will visit your store to get shoes that suit their tastes. You have certainly developed a solid relationship that could turn into a long-term interaction.

Have you also thought about the case that the customer was not satisfied with the services? She would have portrayed your store as one to avoid or would never have posted your product on social media, which completely detracts from the brand's authority.

A bad customer experience = lost customers.

PLANNING THE CUSTOMER'S JOURNEY

NAILING FIRST CONTACT

To get the customer journey right, you have to get every interaction right from the start. This means establishing a solid foundation from the first moment a customer makes contact with your brand. To do this, factors such as clarity, effectiveness, and tone and sentiment must be carefully optimized. Your brand message must be clearly aligned with your actions to leave a positive and lasting impression.

CREATE AN EXPERIENCE THAT TRANSLATES INTO LOYALTY

When you successfully build relationships with customers, you create a positive shopping experience that customers want to repeat. This translates into increased satisfaction and loyalty, recommendations to friends and family, higher purchase frequency, increased average purchase price, and even a possible reduction in the number of returns.

So the goal of marketing is now to give customers and prospects what they want when they want it. Offers must be timely, messages must be relevant, and all personalization must be based on behavior or purchase history extracted from data.

There's a word for that: analytics. And that's a strength of a well-executed integrated marketing management environment.

The following steps detail how harmonic marketing management can be used to bring together analytics, creative development, and campaign execution to create a valuable customer experience.

Analysis Phase

Through the analysis phase, the marketer can look at all the data points that can contribute to understanding customer behavior, including:

- What was purchased and when
- Which channel was used
- Whether incentives were a factor
- How much the discount was
- What items were purchased together
- Which, if any, items were returned
- What were the reasons for the return
- How shopper behavior can influence recommendations to others
- Store location, demographics, and geographic data

Questions like these have given rise to a new type of business intelligence function: the data scientist. It's no longer enough to simply examine data; the data scientist also explores customer relationships to understand who influences them. With that combined knowledge, marketers can deliver more effective and relevant customer messages.

Grocery stores and drug stores do this very well and

offer coupons for frequently purchased items based on history. In the end, it is this type of analysis that drives the relationship parameters (channel preference, brand preference, product combinations, thresholds for incentives, etc.) to create and deliver an incentive that is highly valued by the consumer.

Planning and Operational Phase

Once you have analyzed your customer data, you will have the basis for planning the tactics of your upcoming campaigns. If your goal is personal customer acquisition, harmonic customer journey management can help you coordinate decisions such as:

- Number of campaigns for the year
- Which are the best campaign formats (email, direct mail, mobile, or a combination)
- What the promotional calendar will look like and what steps are required for each campaign before the marketing department can hit send
- Budget for each campaign
- Based on customer history or preferences, which channels to use
- What graphics will be used
- Which agencies will be needed
- Segments to be targeted
- Role of social media in the mix

Execution Phase

Once the analysis has been performed, and the creative has been developed and reviewed, the execution phase begins. Here, your HM environment can be used to implement the planned segmentation and begin delivery of the campaign. Automation tools can help you to:

- deliver personalized messages and relevant offers,
- ensure messages are delivered on time to avoid coupon expiration dates, missed holiday sales, or other windows of opportunity,
- track responses to measure campaign success rate and allow you to stop or potentially redirect an underperforming campaign,
- allow you to demonstrate your knowledge of a customer and continue to build that relationship,
- Continuing the process of refining your customer insight, the campaign results are returned to the analytics group to mine the data once again for new trends, new insights, and to potentially course correct an underperforming campaign.

Customers Demand the Experience that HM Integration Makes Possible

Customers crave the kind of interactions that can occur when the marketer is given the space to build relationships, drive loyalty, and improve satisfaction. But the reverse is also true. The lack of integrated phases can lead to breakdowns that create bottlenecks and, in turn, create delays and increase the likelihood of mistakes, such as undeliverable emails or direct mail. Over time, this can be disastrous for customer satisfaction levels, as too many bad experiences or repeated mistakes will lead to attrition and ultimately lower revenues and profits.

HOW TO IMPROVE THE CUSTOMER'S JOURNEY

Improving the customer journey involves knowing the gaps in your customer service delivery and focusing your efforts on providing the desired customer experience at each stage of the sales funnel. Here are the steps to make your customer journey awesome.

1. **Respond to customer concerns upfront.**

Customer feedback on the experiences they have with your brand is a useful piece of information that you can use to solve their problems effectively. Gathering feedback also allows you to see an outsider's perspective on your sales process. It tells you what challenges your customers may face when they try to make a purchase. By correcting these challenges, you avoid buyer pitfalls and improve the customer experience.

One way to understand what potential customers' concerns may be is to consider what types of questions you would add to something like a website's FAQ page. The purpose of an FAQ page is to answer questions in advance that may hinder the buying process, so you can use the same concept throughout your content. This could involve creating an FAQ page directly, but you could also do things like sharing case studies or explaining your services in a video.

The key factor is that you answer questions early so that a question doesn't turn into a complaint.

2. **Offer assistance.**

The only reason most of us still prefer physical stores

to buy certain products is the assistance we receive. We know that if we are not able to choose the right size, there is someone to help us make the right decision. If we can't find a certain product we have seen on the internet or we are not sure about its quality, we always have someone by our side to answer all the questions.

Not only does timely purchasing assistance help us make the right decision, it often leads us to buy more than we intended. The reason is that when we receive assistance in making an informed purchase, we see the value that the brand offers us, and we are more willing to instantly try more products from their range. This is simple consumer psychology and can also be used in an online business.

You can avoid hijacking the online customer journey by brands that are willing to jump in to steal your customers with live chat/support. A live chat allows your shoppers to leave a quick message the moment they need more information about a product they are interested in. You can take the opportunity to guide them on how to make a purchase, offering information or even recommending alternatives if it doesn't suit their needs.

Some things to keep in mind when using live chat include:

- Make sure it is easy to initiate a chat.
- Make sure the live chat is clearly visible—use a notice if necessary.
- Mention the hours of operation and after hours to set the right expectations.
- Use the chat to offer solutions and recommendations, but keep it brief.
- Be sure to add a human touch to your responses.
- Ask the buyer to sign up with a social account

or share an email address to start a chat and build your lists.

3. **Optimize the customer experience.**

A great benefit of using a CRM is that because it automates all the marketing processes and stores everything in one place. When you have all the analytics and can see the entire customer journey, that's how you can optimize everything. Maybe you get common questions about an aspect of your product or service that you hadn't considered before. Or maybe there's a particular piece of content that your prospects really enjoy. In either case, you'll know the answer to how to improve the process, because all the information is easily accessible.

4. **Personalize content.**

Depending on the scale and scope of your business, "personalize" can have many different meanings. Personalizing your customers' experiences can help create a bond between brand and shopper. For example, offering vouchers to the customer after their first purchase can personalize their experience and build loyalty against the competition.

Personalization doesn't have to be just a discount, but can take many forms:

- Thank-you letters or emails to customers after purchase
- Customer follow-up surveys
- Dynamic offers on the website based on user preferences

Making the customer feel valued even after the sale is made is a great way to improve the overall customer experience.

5. **Audit the customer experience from multiple internal perspectives.**

Since the customer journey is affected by all facets of your business, it's imperative that you don't focus on just one department when conducting a customer-experience audit. As we briefly mentioned earlier, customers interact in some way with every part of your company, so to get a complete picture of the customer experience, you'll need to consider the unique perspective of each of your internal departments. Here are three to get you going:

Marketing

Your marketing team is most likely focused on customer acquisition, so they'll have the best perspective on brand awareness and user expectations. They will know what content your visitors consume the most and what will generate the most qualified leads. Surveying your marketing team will help you understand how people are finding your business and what you can do to better shape your reputation before a sale.

Sales

The sales department will have information about the early stages of the customer relationship. They are on the front line with the customer and their interactions reveal what really motivates potential customers. Sales team members have information about the challenges customers encounter on a daily basis and how they expect your product or service to solve those obstacles. For leads that don't convert into customers, your sales team can help you understand what it is about your product offering that caused them to miss that opportunity.

Customer Service

It's important to know that what you're communicating in your sales and marketing processes aligns with your customers' actual experiences. Your customer service and success team can provide insight into this reality, as they are often the first line of communication for product feedback and frustration. They hear candid customer feedback on a daily basis, so welcome their perspective on what is causing your customers the most problems.

For example, they can tell you what questions are asked most during support calls and what topics in your feedback forums generate the most activity. In SaaS (Software As A Service) companies, the support team does the most work with the user interface, so surveying their opinions about the product can be a good way to address technical pain points.

6. **Distribute customer experience data to your entire team.**

If you want to get the entire company on board with your shiny new customer experience plan, it's important that everyone has access to your findings. Keeping your employees aware of the conclusions you've drawn from your research will help your team optimize day-to-day internal processes, such as customer routing, workflow automation, and customer tagging. Not only that, but distributing customer insights throughout the company can help as well.

Address Customer Needs Faster

According to Meta SaaS, 31 percent of SaaS licenses end up unused, making it even more important to address customer issues as quickly as possible. Having data on where your customers are likely to encounter roadblocks will help your team avoid user frustration and smooth out any pain points in the customer journey.

Improve Product/Service Quality

As mentioned above, your customer service or success team will be able to provide feedback on how usability issues with your product or service are affecting the overall customer experience. If your success team leaders and contributors meet with your product team, you can review the top support ticket categories to identify the most common usability-related issues.

Increase Sales Opportunities

Your sales team will find it easier to identify upsell opportunities because they will have a better understanding of the best time to reach out to customers. They can identify specific opportunities in the customer's timeline to reach out with reengagement initiatives (such as a product add-on) that can increase overall revenue over time.

7. Learn from customer churn when it occurs.

According to a Bain & Company study, if you can generate a 5 percent increase in customer retention, you can increase your company's profits by 25 percent to 95 percent. A good way to start is to use an application's analytics to analyze areas of the customer experience where there is low engagement.

Low engagement usually suggests a higher risk of

customer churn. It will help you create an engagement correlation that can help you identify which customers are at the highest risk of churn. You can use user application analytics to determine the engagement percentage that will result in the highest likelihood of churn, and then set up a monitoring system to alert your customer success team if a customer approaches that value. This gives your team the opportunity to proactively reach out to resolve an issue before it's too late.

Even for customers you can't stop from leaving, be sure to find out why they decided to switch. Offer multiple channels for customers to leave feedback and take their opinions seriously. If you are truly focused on creating a better experience for your customer, you should want to know about instances where your company fell short. Make it easy for the customer to cancel their account, but leverage your success team to find out exactly why this customer decided to cancel.

8. Consider the customer experience with UX/UI design.

Think about where the customer experience begins. Before a potential customer reaches a customer service representative, they will do their own research before formally asking for help. It is imperative that your company's website is easy to navigate and clear in its offerings. Eighty-eight percent of users are less likely to return to a website after a bad user experience. To prevent the customer experience from becoming complicated, have your engineers or marketing team optimize your digital domain to deliver an engaging and informative experience so that the customer journey starts on a positive note.

9. Engage with customers all the time.

The story doesn't end there. Even your most loyal followers would like to know how they can get more benefits from your product. The good news is that you can kill two birds with one stone by engaging with your customers and prospects and improving brand awareness through influencer marketing.

While content marketing and email marketing are two topics that many people have written about, I think it would be unfair if I didn't highlight some invaluable systematic techniques that can improve your customers' experience. It really doesn't matter if you have a SaaS company or if your business is in interior design and furniture sales—you can always improve and overcome industry limitations.

If you know the toughest problems your visitors are facing, you can leverage your data and come up with a few step-by-step guidelines, beginner's guides, or how-to articles to help them solve their problems without paying a dime. This will not only differentiate your company from your competitors, but it will also create a sense of ownership about your business in your customers.

In case you haven't collected this data, you can start today by conducting a quick survey and sharing it with your subscribers and customers. The quickest solution is to let your customers, visitors, and prospects know that you are giving gifts in exchange for their honest opinion. This is a win-win situation and helps you quickly build your database and learn what you need to correct. Once you have gathered the right information, you can plan your engagement strategies.

Ultimately, if you want to be in business for the long

term and outperform your competitors, you need to know that your most valuable assets are your customers. Believe me, if you plan your customer journey experience based on reliable facts, you will get happy customers that drive more leads and referrals.

CASE STUDIES

STARBUCKS: GAMIFIED LOYALTY PROGRAM

The company's awesome gamified loyalty system allows you to collect stars when purchasing your favorite drinks and get exciting rewards in return. The awesome app features, the great user experience, and the innovative gamification approach are excellent ways to drive more sales, gain more brand visibility, and keep customers satisfied.

To drive even more engagement, Starbucks also gives you the opportunity to get stars faster with additional challenges and Double Star Days. You can also order on the go before arriving to your local coffee shop!

The way they've designed their reward system not only gets more revenue for the company but also offers an outstanding customer experience. In fact, The Starbucks Reward Loyalty Program currently has more than sixteen million members, driving 40 percent of the total sales of the company.

The company's successful gamification approach is one of the best customer experience examples showing that, with some additional incentives that translate to tangible rewards, you can:

- incentivize more product purchases,
- encourage returning visits,

- get valuable customer data,
- as well as promote merchandise and partner offers.

AMAZON: PRODUCT EXPERIENCE ONLINE

Amazon—the customer feedback champion and one of the largest e-commerce platforms in the world. Apart from setting the standards in e-commerce with competitive prices and unrivaled product inventory, the company is also one of the biggest references when it comes to digital product experience.

From a Google-like ability to search to extremely detailed product education, Amazon makes it easy for customers to evaluate if a product fits their needs. They have an extremely powerful system for customer reviews and ratings that help you learn more about a particular product. Customers who have previously purchased the product can also upload images with it, and you can easily translate their reviews to your native language as well.

The company also provides a handy recommendation system to help you understand which product might fit your needs the best. It is based on previous search terms or what additional products other users have bought along with the one you are evaluating. And what's even more awesome, you can even rate the reviews of other users to let everyone know if they have been helpful to you.

CHAPTER 3 WORKSHEET

THE AIDA MODEL

We are now ready to launch our message, and to do it in a harmonic way, we must follow some patterns and take into account everything we have learned in the previous topics. Let's practice with the AIDA model we learned in Chapter 3. Think of a possible campaign you want to launch and, keeping in mind the examples seen in the chapter, complete the following chart.

THE AIDA MODEL	
ATTENTION **How will I grab the reader's attention?**	
INTEREST **How will I pique their interest so they'll be open to what I'm offering?**	
DESIRE **How will I make them strongly desire my offering—whether a blog post, consulting service, or software product?**	
ACTION **What's my powerful call to action? Start by thinking about this and then work backward.**	

Now take everything you have outlined in the previous section and try to write a piece of copy that brings together the most important points established with the AIDA model. Remember:

1. Write for your buyer persona
2. Be credible
3. Think of a creative title

Empowering your audience with useful, informative, or fun resources can make all the difference. Spend some time focusing on your content and start dreaming up new ideas on the following page.

....

....

....

....

....

....

....

....

Now let's create a customer journey. Meet with your team and think through your customer experience together. What are the moments that matter in your interactions? When can you make the biggest impact?

....

....

....

....

....

....

....

....

....

....

....

It is time to create our customer map. Complete the following sheet, taking into account the following points:

- *Touch Points*: What are the key steps in your service process?
- *Team Tasks*: What are your staff and volunteers doing at each step of the way? Who does the client come into contact with?
- *Customer Actions*: What are customers doing at each step of the way? What decisions and actions are they responsible for?
- *Questions/Barriers*: What uncertainties does the client face? Is there language or jargon the client not understand? What gets in their way?
- *Motivations/Needs*: What will keep people moving through the process? What information, benefits, motions, values, etc. will help them move forward?
- *Gaps*: What's missing right now from the process for the client? For the team?
- *Possible Improvements*: What improvements can be made to the process, the structure, the information to address the gaps and barriers to an exceptional experience?

....

....

....

....

....

....

....

....

....

....

....

....

....

What have you learned about your service process that could make a difference in the quality of the experience for your clients and your team? Write it down.

....

....

....

....

....

....

....

....

....

....

....

CHAPTER 4

HARMONIC BUSINESS DEVELOPMENT

No company can afford not to move forward. It may be at the top of the heap today but at the bottom of the heap tomorrow, if it doesn't.

—James Cash Penney, JCPenney

Business development is a term that often can be quite unclear and changes in meaning depending on who you're talking to. Almost everyone is familiar with the basic functions of different teams across an organization—sales, engineering, finance, etc. However, when it comes to "biz dev," there is a level of ambiguity surrounding the true meaning of the term and what responsibilities individuals with the title have.

Business development refers to the multidisciplinary management for the definition of products and services, aimed at strengthening their commercialization. It is important to define new opportunities, creation of needs, and design of an alliance strategy; this includes brainstorming new ideas, initiatives, and activities to increase profitability. The goal of business development is not just to increase profits, the goal is to make intelligent business decisions that create value for organizations and customers. In this sense, the business development manager defines how the business must evolve in order not to stagnate but to continue growing.

It is very common to confuse business development with marketing or sales. It is important to know that, although there must be a close synergy between them, they are totally different areas, each with its own functions. Let's say that business development goes ahead of the rest of the areas defining the strategies for the progress of the business, taking advantage of the opportunities of the environment, or creating them, as well as establishing the necessary synergies with external entities.

WHAT DOES A BUSINESS DEVELOPMENT DEPARTMENT DO?

1. *Identify and seize opportunities.*

It must identify and take advantage of the opportunities provided by the environment, such as markets with high potential that have not yet been exploited, either the extension into new geographic areas or the development of new products and/or services. In addition, it must have the ability to create opportunities that lead to business growth, anticipating market movements.

2. *Create opportunities if there are none.*

Business development must have the ability to create

opportunities that lead to business growth, even ahead of market movements. Go one step ahead.

3. *Establish synergies.*

For business growth, it is necessary to establish strategic alliances with external entities, either to expand into new geographical areas, develop new products and/or services, new suppliers to reinforce the current business value chain, develop new processes, etc. Synergies with third parties are a key element in the evolution of any business.

4. *Innovate.*

The business development department must go hand in hand with innovation, both in technology and business processes. This is of great relevance nowadays, due to the constant and rapid evolution of technology and society. To remain static in the face of these changes is to allow oneself to be knocked down in the market war to which companies are subjected today.

5. *Ask the questions no one else is asking.*

Business development must go beyond reality, beyond habit, beyond routine. It must always look into how to do things differently, how to improve current processes. Think that everything can be improved and that no procedure is written in stone.

6. *Define the strategy.*

As always, strategy is a must. Through the strategy, business development defines how the business will evolve, always considering the corporate objectives, as well as the mission and vision of the company. Without a strategy, it is practically impossible to obtain results, since only improvised actions will be carried out without pursuing a common goal.

It is vital that the activities carried out by this department are framed in a work methodology and a business development plan with well-defined objectives, aligned with the organizational objectives, values, and global strategy of the company, thus avoiding improvisation that can lead to mistakes that can damage the company.

In today's changing market, it is essential to have a business development department that is 100 percent focused on seeking opportunities for evolution and defining strategies to adapt to changes quickly and even anticipate them. In this way, the company advances at the speed of the markets.

Sales versus Business Development

Although both sales and business development are aimed at growing new business, the two functions differ greatly and serve different purposes.

Earlier in this chapter we learned that business development is essential to the sales process. The business development team is responsible for moving qualified leads through the sales funnel, but it doesn't close deals on its own.

That's where sales come in. The sales team's primary function is to generate revenue. Sales reps are responsible for demonstrating the product, making negotiations, and ultimately closing the deal. Converting leads into customers is much easier to achieve when sales and business development work together to streamline the sales process.

Separating these two functions within a company allows each team to specialize in their specific role and help grow the business more efficiently.

Both functions require a similar set of skills, allowing professional development opportunities for business development representatives who want to move into a closing position later on. The relationship-building skills learned in the business development position are easily transferable and lay the foundation for the skills needed to succeed in sales, marketing, or even customer success.

Many business development teams function as a subset of the sales department and are driven by similar metrics. Next, we'll look at how to measure business development success.

Measuring the Impact of Business Development Efforts

The sales metrics of a business development team are going to vary depending on what a company's sales cycle looks like. Since the primary function of this role is to generate new sales opportunities, one of the easiest ways to quantify this data is to look at the Business Development Representative (BDR) influenced sales pipeline, or the number of potential deals created as a result of business development efforts.

Many BDR teams have quotas that align with the company's overall revenue goals. To meet revenue targets (which fall on the shoulders of the sales team), business development must consistently generate a good order backlog.

Although metrics vary by company, the most common ways to track BDR activity are prospecting activities (cold calls and outbound emails), the number of appointments made, and the number of sales pipelines generated. All this data is typically stored and tracked using CRM software.

WHERE DOES MARKETING FIT IN?

While it may not seem like there is much alignment between marketing and business development, it is important that both teams are in sync and work together to achieve the common goal: to grow the business.

Marketing's primary responsibility is to promote the brand and establish a presence in the marketplace. This is achieved through various communication strategies (content marketing, advertising, public relations, etc.) and is measured in different ways. The key marketing metric that links to business development is lead generation.

The BDR team relies on marketing to generate high-quality leads, and marketing expects business development to nurture those leads and convert them into sales opportunities. Strategic alignment between the two teams is key to fueling long-term sales flow and helping the business grow.

There is no single definition of business development. However, knowing the basics is the first step in understanding exactly what these "business development" people do and how it all fits into the big picture of a growing organization. To achieve our goal of harmonizing each and every aspect of our brand, it is necessary to understand the importance of each of these departments to our business mission.

HOW TO NETWORK AND BUILD RELATIONSHIPS

Relationship-building activity in business is quite different from personal relationship building. However, business relationships have some similarities that clearly require good interpersonal and communication skills. When it comes time to expand a business network, it takes a bit of planning and design to affect relationship-building activities smoothly. To learn how to build a relationship of this nature, a number of precursors must be defined. These include:

- The visibility of the existing business
- The company's reputation and brand
- Type of target market
- Importance of the company as part of an online and offline community

HOW TO BUILD A BUSINESS RELATIONSHIP

Networking is defined by a number of inclusive elements. These can be business and industry partners, a loyal clientele, links to community organizations, and a well-structured public relations plan. To learn how to build a relationship, a company must first study the "reflection in the mirror" of the company's corporate image. What does that reflection say about the company—is it customer-friendly or somewhat aloof and indifferent? The importance of the steps in learning how to build a business relationship can be a catalyst for further expansion of the business network.

When we talk about professional networking, we are referring to a technique based on the acquisition of contacts by a company, which are usually other companies or professionals with common interests, in order to create collaborations that help to take advantage of new opportunities in the short, medium, and long term.

We could say that networking focuses on expanding a company's contact agenda, something that is essential today for the growth of any business, as it allows the creation of agreements and collaborations with professionals from different sectors.

Advantages of Business Networking

Networking offers the possibility of meeting new professionals that could be useful for your company in the future, helping you to achieve certain objectives.

Among the main benefits that professional networking offers to a company, it is worth mentioning the attraction of new employees to incorporate to your work team, as well as the possibility of looking for new investors and/or financing formulas.

It could be considered that SMEs and start-ups are the great beneficiaries of professional networking, since these practices help them to find allies in their business growth.

Main advantages of networking for your company are:

- **Increase your visibility**: Networking will help you to make your company known among different specialists and professionals in the sector.
- **Exchange knowledge**: You will be able to share knowledge with other professionals and improve the training of your professionals.
- **Increase your contact list**: By meeting other

professionals, you will be able to add them to your contact list and call on them when necessary.

- **Create collaborations**: With networking, you will be able to establish possible synergies or collaborations with other companies or professionals.
- **Get new investors or partners**: If you need to obtain financing, networking events will help you find new investors and/or partners to support your project.
- **Exchange services** with other professionals.
- **Improve your business**: By publicizing your products or services, you will receive opinions from qualified and experienced people that will help you improve them to meet your goals.
- **Better knowledge of the market**: By keeping in touch with professionals, you will be able to know the market better and have an overview of the state it is in.
- **Expand your staff**: You will meet new professionals that you may be able to add to your staff, making it more competitive.

Keys to Professional Networking

1. *Be clear about your objectives.*

Having clear objectives is key to getting the most out of professional networking, as it will help you to know who you want to contact and what you want to convey to them. You will also know which events you are most interested in attending.

Before networking, it is important to have a defined strategy of what you want to do and the objectives you want to achieve since it is not the same to want to increase your visibility as a brand, as it is to look for professionals to help you in a specific area.

2. *Be useful to others.*

Although the purpose of networking is to obtain new opportunities for your company, you will also have to be useful to others, since it should not be forgotten that it is a "two-way street" in which everyone should win.

You must be able to convey that your company is of interest to other professionals in the industry, as this will make it easier for you to cross-pollinate interests.

3. *Take advantage of social networks.*

Social networks have favored the practice of networking, so you should give it the importance it deserves. If you have a good network of contacts in the main social networks, it will be easier for you to generate impact and capture the attention of other professionals.

Without a doubt, maintaining good activity in social networks is one of the best ways of networking.

4. *Attend events.*

You must be aware that today, in any business event, you can perform professional networking, so it is important that you stay active and go to business events where you have the opportunity to network—as long as they are related to your field. That is, if you have a start-up in which you create applications for scanning documents with your cell phone, obviously it is not necessary to attend a networking event on horse training. But if it is related to your sector, clear your agenda and go to it. Especially if it is at a national level, organized by an important company, or attended by experts in a field that interests you. In these cases it is essential that you go because the quality of the contacts you can get is worth any effort. But do not neglect local events. Creating a network of contacts in your immediate environment is also important.

Networking is not a one-time action, but a long-distance race in which you must set yourself a series of long-term goals, gaining new contacts that will help you achieve them.

5. *Pay attention and listen.*

Unless you or your company is one of the highlights of the networking event, our advice is to listen more than talk. It's okay if you ask questions from time to time or interject some interesting information to make yourself known, but in general, it's best to pay attention. This helps you to get to know people better and generates stronger bonds.

6. *Keep in touch.*

Because all the work is useless if, once the event is over, they never hear from you again. Relationships are like a plant—you have to take care of them a little bit every day to keep them healthy and strong. So, from time to time, send an email or comment on their social media or blog. The important thing is to show them that you don't forget about them and that you care about keeping in touch.

Mistakes that Ruin Your Networking

Now that you know how you should act, it's time to tell you what you should never do under any circumstances.

1. *Do not offer anything in return.*

As we remarked in its definition, networking is based on all parties getting a benefit. So make sure you always give something in return. If your mentality is to receive without giving, you're wasting your time.

2. *Look desperate.*

No matter how much your idol comes to you and you want to "connect" with them (or with a company that is a benchmark in your industry), it's never a good idea to come across as desperate. Or would you accept someone into your network with that attitude?

3. *Being overconfident.*

Just as it's bad to act desperate, it's also bad to appear overconfident. Don't get me wrong, most people like people who are confident in themselves or their product, but too much of it can be interpreted negatively. Especially because it is often accompanied by a more aggressive way of acting and that drives away potential contacts. The same happens if you are a small company and you try to connect with a giant in your sector that almost acts as a monopolist. Also, size doesn't always mean better networking partner and maybe a smaller one is better for your business.

4. *The problems with business cards.*

Specifically two: handing out too many and not carrying any (as you can see, the two extremes). In the first case, although we said earlier that the idea is the more contacts the better, you should not interpret it as handing out business cards left and right. There is a middle ground between just talking to one person and the whole event having a card from you, and your obligation is to find it. And, believe it or not, in the twenty-first century, business cards are still a great way to exchange contact information, so don't even think about going without them.

5. *Not showing your talent.*

Despite recommending that you keep a low profile, that doesn't mean being invisible. And if at some point the opportunity arises to show your talent, don't be afraid to do so. Companies love to work with talented people. But the event isn't the only place to show what you know. If you have a website or social media, you are obligated to showcase your talent there for everyone to see.

6. *Leaving all the work to social media.*

And speaking of social networks, one of the most common mistakes when it comes to making a networking strategy is to think that Facebook, Instagram, Twitter, etc.

will do the work for you. If you think that by creating a profile on them and sharing something from time to time you will get a lot of requests for networking, you are very wrong. It is obvious that they are an indispensable element to achieve it, but they are one more resource and, by themselves, are not enough.

Professional networking is essential for a company to add new contacts to its agenda and to take advantage of them to create new business opportunities in the future.

It is an increasingly common practice in the business world, which is carried out in all kinds of events and congresses and that favor collaboration between different professionals with a mutual objective.

Study the tips on building relationships and the activities that promote better business relationships between clients, vendors, and business networks. With a little effort, expenditure of time, and dedicated funding, businesses find they enjoy a greatly expanded business network for the long term.

HOW TO GET NEW CLIENTS

In a perfect world, you would have an unlimited budget to market your business to find new customers and increase sales. You could buy lots of online and offline advertising, run promotions to generate in-store and online traffic, and launch a proactive public relations campaign to increase visibility and awareness of your product or brand. But this is not a perfect world. Realistically, most small businesses, and even many medium-sized ones, have more great ideas on how to sell their products than they have resources available.

So where do you start if you're looking for more

customers? Learning how to generate new sales opportunities is an essential skill for an entrepreneur. Even if you don't consider yourself a salesman in the classic sense of Willy Loman's character from Arthur Miller's play *Death of a Salesman*, you must understand that the possibilities for finding new customers range from cold calling names from the phone book to buying lists of potential customers to using the latest internet techniques, such as search engine optimization, to drive new business to your website.

Let's assume that if you have reached this part of the book you already know very well who your potential customer is, how your customers relate to you, and what your value proposition is. You will also have done market research and know your competitors' strengths and weaknesses, as well as your own. Certain products and services may appeal to one audience but not another, so it is critical to understand the strengths, weaknesses, opportunities, and threats of your target market.

Make sure you know who the gatekeepers and influencers are; they will affect the decision-makers and you will most likely have to sell to them differently than to the end-user. For example, parents may be gatekeepers for products aimed at children or CTOs may have influence on a company's decision to invest in new software.

Determine what key messages, features, and benefits are important to each potential market. Explain to these customers how your company can help them solve their problems. In order for a customer to come to your online store, you have to find a reason why these customers want to come to you. You have to clearly explain the value proposition.

Next, you need to figure out where to reach these

customers and whether there should be a marketing or advertising plan that goes along with that outreach.

There are a variety of old techniques and new tools you can use to find new customers and increase sales. It is best to understand the range of options you have to determine which can best help your business reach new customers. Newspaper readers may not be attracted to internet-based sales techniques. Similarly, business owners who are used to hiring only people they know may be more attracted to a meeting at the chamber of commerce than a blind invitation to connect on LinkedIn or Facebook.

The following is a summary of the available techniques:

Cold calling. This is telemarketing without the call center. This is a blind contact with a potential customer who is not expecting a proposal. Leads can be obtained by consulting blog articles or magazine articles, lists of potential customers compiled by third parties, or by paying attention to people or companies that travel to your territory.

Networking. This can be done the old-fashioned way, by participating in community organizations such as the chamber of commerce, or by attending business functions such as trade shows. Social functions—dinner invitations, book clubs, award ceremonies, business tradeshows, charity galas, golf and tennis tournaments, networking groups, conferences, etc.—can also lead to potential business. All of these things are important ways to network to find new customers. Networking has also taken a turn into the twenty-first century on the internet, with the rise in popularity of websites such as LinkedIn, Facebook, and Plaxo. Many companies are finding that this type of networking, making contacts through friends or former colleagues, can lead to new customers.

Get advocates for your products. Use business contacts who have been satisfied with your products to help you generate referrals and recommendations. Once you have sold to them, customers can help you sell to others by offering positive testimonials and leveraging a refer-a-friend campaign created by your company. This technique also employs word-of-mouth marketing. Help customers help you by giving them the ammunition they need to tell your story to others. Don't be afraid to ask, "Is there someone else I can talk to who we can also help?"

Affiliate marketing. Look for noncompeting products or services that reach the same audience to see if there are ways to collaborate through shared outreach efforts, such as newsletters, mailings (online and offline), or co-branding opportunities. You may be able to uncover a handful of like-minded products or services that target your customers. Propose to the owners of these companies that they support each other. Your customers will see the joint efforts as a value-added opportunity to reinforce their choice of brands.

Leverage your website. Today there are all kinds of tools with which you can attract new potential customers to your website. Search engine optimization (SEO)—the use of keywords and other techniques to get your site on the first page of search engines—has become an art. There are websites, such as Search Engine Watch, that will keep you up to date on SEO techniques. In addition, there are a growing number of paid SEO consultants who can help you use all the tricks and techniques to improve your search results. You can also use a variety of blogs, chat rooms, podcasts, and webinars to get the word out about your website and your company. A website is a dynamic tool, not a one-time experience. The major search engines constantly update their algorithms, so monitor your website regularly to make sure your keywords are leading you to customers. Be sure to keep your website updated with fresh content to keep your customers coming back often for more.

Advertising. Typically, businesses are recommended to spend 3 to 5 percent of their revenue on advertising, but a small business needs to make sure that advertising is effective. One way to do that is to ask your customers where they have heard about you so you can gauge your effectiveness. In addition, you have to carefully choose the markets in which you advertise to make sure you reach your target audience. If you're targeting an older audience, local publications ads may be the way to go. But if you're targeting Generation X or Y, it may be better to advertise online or on streaming services. You need to define your demographic before developing your advertising or marketing plan.

Promotions. No matter what your niche market is, there is always room to surprise customers with some kind of promotion. Whenever you do a promotion, spread it to all your customers and make it somehow reach potential customers who never bought from your company. Just be careful to calculate beforehand if the discount may negatively affect your cash flow and hinder the profitability of your campaign.

Email Listing. Building a strong and qualified email list is one of the best marketing investments your business can make. This channel is very powerful for cultivating and engaging an audience. Email marketing still has the advantage of being a widely tested communication medium and not suffering from major changes over time. The same cannot be said for social media, which can change its internal policies at any time and affect your entire marketing plan. With the right actions, your email list can be the key to generating a lot of leads and bringing many customers to your business.

Corporate blog. The blog is at the center of the Inbound Marketing methodology, the main digital way to attract and retain customers today. This method basically consists of generating value through relevant content for the buyer persona. In this way, the more you help your potential customers—even before trying to sell them something—the better.

Where does the blog come into all this? It is the main content channel that your company may want, and the best part, its implementation and maintenance cost can be cost effective.

HOW TO GET NEW JV PARTNERS

Like it or not, some companies need a collaborative mindset to succeed. You have to step out of your comfort zone, look at the industry as a whole, and ask yourself:

Who can I partner with to achieve my business goal?
Who is a good fit?
What are the benefits and risks?

This is what a joint venture (JV) is all about. It is **an agreement between two companies to work together to achieve a certain business objective**. It could be attracting new customers, entering new markets, or helping to launch a new product—whatever. So joint ventures can be really powerful in helping your small business grow quickly.

Now let's look at how to form a joint venture. The process you'll undertake to identify the right joint venture partners and how to put your plan into action.

Types of Joint Venture Relationships

Joint ventures come in two main forms:

1. *Cooperate with another company with limits.*

This is an agreement to collaborate with another company with limits and specifications. For example, you have launched a promising product and a larger company wants to distribute it to a larger market. You can agree to form a joint venture on a contract basis.

2. *Create an independent joint venture.*

If you want to take things to the next level, you can create a separate joint venture, with each party owning a percentage of shares and agreeing on how the company should operate or function.

Now, how can you decide between the two? Start thinking about these things:

What is your goal? Do you want to create a joint venture with limitations? Or are you open to flexibility?
How much protection do you want for your business?
How much money can you spend on building this relationship?
When you make the decision, think about the pros and cons: What happens next if the venture is a

big success? What if it goes wrong? How much risk are you willing to take?

If you still have doubts, don't rush; seek legal advice from a professional. They will give you advice on how a joint venture might affect your business specifically and how much profit you stand to gain or lose from it.

Where to Find JV Partners

1. *Your own network*

People in your own network are a good starting point because they already know, like, and trust you. This could be family, friends, colleagues, people you meet through associations or networking events, etc. Even if they are not a potential joint venture partner, reach out to your friends and colleagues to see if they can recommend someone who is a good fit.

2. *Your mentors*

You shouldn't take it for granted that your coach or mentor will promote you (unless that's part of the deal) and, of course, it may not be a good fit based on your niche and theirs. But it doesn't hurt to reach out to them and ask them to support you in any way they can. For example, they might send you an email to introduce you to someone who is a good fit for you. Don't forget that your mentors want to see you succeed.

3. *Clients*

Another group with whom you have already established trust is your customers. You'd be surprised how many of your clients are already promoting you. And if they knew they could get paid for doing so, it's a real win-win. So let your satisfied customers know how to sign up as an affiliate partner. Some of those customers will be suitable to become joint venture partners for you as well.

4. *Social networking*

Social networks are one of the best places to connect with potential joint venture partners. Before you approach them, make sure you know them and their work. That means getting on their list. Check out what they're passionate about, what they work on, and how they promote themselves. That way, when you reach out to them, you can make a real connection. So instead of just sending a connection request, send a personal message to let them know what you love most about what they do.

And remember that it must come from a place of service. Tell them what you like about what they do and that you'd like to connect to learn more about how you can support them. Then, be sure to follow through!

5. *Live events*

Some of the best joint venture partners are people you meet at live events. There's something really powerful about sitting next to someone and sharing a cup of tea or a meal. Just make sure you follow up because you know as well as I do that live events can get you excited, but it's when you go home that the real work takes place.

6. *Telesummits and giveaway events*

One of my favorite ways to connect with potential joint venture partners is through telesummits and gifting events. If you participate in a telesummit or giveaway event as a contributor, then reach out to the other contributors and get to know them. If you are new and not yet established as a contributor, contact the people who organize these events and let them know that you would be happy to support their event. You can offer to do an interview, give an extra gift, or even just promote the event.

How do you find these events in the first place? You'll probably see them promoted on social media or on other people's lists. You can also Google "telesummit" and words relevant to your niche. Even if that event has already happened, contact the organizer. Chances are they will be doing other events in the future.

Once you have found some suitable candidates, answer these questions:

- What kind of reputation do they have?
- Do they already have joint venture partnerships?
- Do you have any idea how they manage and run the business?
- Are they financially secure?
- Can you trust them?

Before entering into an agreement, it is very important that you protect your company's interests. Certainly, trust is an important factor in this partnership, but you need to make sure they are worthy of your trust.

Approach Your Potential Joint Venture Partner

Have you already found your ideal joint venture partner? Now it's a question of compatibility. You also need to do your part by showing your potential partner that a joint venture will be a great opportunity for both parties. Here are some tips for closing the deal:

- **Get their attention before you make the proposal**. You don't have to wait until you are ready to make the proposal. Get their attention before you approach them. Do you like their products? Buy some of them. Interested in attending their free workshops and webinars? Sign up and participate. Let them know you exist without expecting anything in return. This is a great way to build a relationship, even before a joint venture occurs.
- **Share some of your complementary resources**. Let's say you've done your research and your potential JV partner lacks some resources that you can provide. If this is the case, go ahead and share your resources with them.
- **Establish a relationship**. If you are in the same industry as your potential joint venture partner, relationship building should be easy and seamless. It's great common ground to start with. When initiating conversations, share related experiences and be yourself. Think of yourself as an acquaintance who wants to know more about someone else.

- **Leverage your assets**. It all starts with research. Find out what assets they don't have and what assets they lack. If your company has the ability to provide them, be sure to leverage those assets to attract a potential JV partner.
- **Personalize your speech**. This is very important. Don't send a predetermined proposal or you won't get anything from your potential JV partner. If you personalize your pitch, they know it's for them. They know you've gone to the trouble of getting to know them and why it might be a great opportunity to join forces. Simply put, personalization gives you a better chance of closing the deal. Talk about the potential partnership through your language. Mention the areas of their business that need help and demonstrate why you are the right person to support them. And make sure this partnership will be mutually beneficial.
- **Draft your joint venture agreement**. Although the law does not require a written contract to create a joint venture, I strongly suggest that you draft one. As with any business transaction, it is important that the terms and conditions of the joint venture be set forth in a written agreement. This ensures that the joint venture partners share the same level of commitment to the agreement.

  First and foremost, it should be understood that the joint venture agreement should be drafted by a legal professional. You can find

preconceived joint venture agreements on the internet, but it is important that they are tailored to your business. Experts should be consulted.
Your draft joint venture agreement should include the following provisions:

- The business objectives of the joint venture
- The type of joint venture
- The share or contribution of each party in the joint venture
- Each party's control and management of the joint venture
- The details of how each party will share profits, losses, and liabilities
- How intellectual property will be used by both parties
- The role of the joint venture's officers and employees
- A confidentiality clause to protect certain trade secrets of both parties to the joint venture
- Dispute mechanism between the parties
- Procedures for termination of the joint venture
- Details of the exit strategy

- Make the joint venture work. If all the terms and conditions set out in the joint venture agreement are settled, it's time for the fun part. You have to know how to manage and handle the relationship.

Here are some tips for building a good joint venture relationship:

- *Give your joint venture partner a good first impression.* It's important to get the relationship off to a good start. Show that you are reliable and willing to help if there are any problems or issues with onboarding.
- *Communicate with your JV partner.* Communication is an essential part of any joint venture relationship. It's a no-brainer. Generally, you should arrange regular, ongoing meetings with the business entities involved in the joint venture. Or, at a minimum, schedule regular virtual meetings if all key people work remotely.
- *Be transparent.* Want to know how to gain the trust of your joint venture partner? Simply be transparent. Be open to sharing information and resources that can make the joint venture successful. Be honest with what you're really trying to accomplish, and aim for the same goals. And if there are any internal problems in your company that could affect the joint venture, let your business partner know as soon as possible. The last thing you want is to make yourself suspect and lose their trust in you.
- *Be open to change.* Whether or not you decide to cooperate with another company, it's still important to be flexible. Take into account the other party's plans and suggestions that can improve the operation of the joint venture,

even if that means you have to implement something new or unique.

- *Be fair*. The most important thing is to be fair. There is no such thing as a perfect joint venture. And I'm telling you that all partnerships can have conflicts. So if a conflict arises with your business partner, deal with it fairly. Propose win-win solutions rather than one-upping the other. Remember that joint ventures are mutually beneficial arrangements. They are not meant just to please you or to make you successful.

Joint ventures can be critical to the success of your business. The resources, assets, skills, or knowledge of other companies can help you scale, boost your reputation, and earn more profit. Make decisions wisely. Choose the type of joint venture that will benefit your business the most. Be sure to choose a joint venture partner who shares the same goals and vision as you do. And while the joint venture agreement is active, do your part to make the partnership work. Achieve the goal with your business partner and it will become a tool for everyone's success.

HOW TO GET NEW REFERRAL PARTNERS

Getting referrals can make or break a business, and there are many ways to get them. Getting satisfied customers who want to recommend you to their friends and family is the bread and butter of any business. But for newer businesses that don't have a large customer base, finding referral partners in a complementary business to yours is a great way to start getting referrals.

The task at hand is how to increase the size of your circle to include more people. To recommend your business, people have to know, like, and trust you. They want to be sure that you will take good care of the clients they send you. To do this, they would like to get to know you better than just hearing your name.

Here are five ways to find your new referral partners:

1. Create a most-wanted list of ten professional categories whose members are in frequent contact with the type of client you want. Know ten people in each profession. Seek them out, meet with them, and familiarize them with your expertise and the benefits of the service you offer. Find out more about what they do and the type of clients they serve so you can refer them to them as well. Share your most-wanted list with others and ask them to introduce you to people they already know.
2. When you fail to make enough connections through networking and those you already have, don't be afraid to seek them out. You can find people in almost any occupation in the local phone book or on the web. If you approach them as a colleague and express your desire for the two of you to help each other become more successful, you will find many people willing to get to know each other better.

3. Eliminate potential referral sources that are not good sources from your list and replace them with more reliable ones. Over time, you may find that some of the people in your circle are not particularly good referral sources. That's to be expected. The reason you want so many names to begin with is that only a few will consistently refer you. You can always add more names later to replace some of the people who don't seem to be as helpful. However, a few consistent referral partners will probably be more than enough to keep you busy.
4. Educate referral partners. Referral partners should know how to recognize a referral opportunity. Provide your referral source with all the information they need to refer ideal clients to you. Your referral partner must have enough knowledge about you for them to promote you. They need to know what you do, what benefits you provide, who your customers are, how to qualify a "suspect," and what your unique selling proposition is. It's your job to teach your referral partners these things. Find ways to share this critical information. One of the best ways is to take them through your advisory process. Inevitably, an advisor's best referral partners are those who are clients of the advisor.
5. Build strong, trustworthy, and reliable relationships to encourage people to refer others to you naturally. To be referred business, people have to know, like, and trust

> you. They want to be sure that you will take good care of the customers they send you. To do this, they would like to get to know you better than just hearing your name. Take the time to cultivate a relationship and develop it over the long term. Listen to your referral partners. Give them time to tell you about their business.

Look for opportunities to help your business. Ask who would be a good reference for your partner and reciprocate when appropriate. Be aware of referrals you can give to your partners. If possible, give the first referral.

Trust is essential to an effective relationship with referral partners. Partners will form an opinion of your trustworthiness by observing your actions. Your referral partner will look at how you treat others, the honesty you show, the integrity you demonstrate, the way you treat them, and those they refer to you. Trust is easily earned and easily lost.

The secret is in finding your strategic alliances. Know the people who know. The professionals who serve your market can be great sources of referrals for a variety of reasons, but to attract these key people, you must know who to look for and what you can offer them.

CASE STUDIES

- **Dropbox** offers free products or services in exchange for users referring new customers. You can earn more cloud storage space in exchange for referring a friend.
- Renewable products manufacturer **Tesla** is

betting that its customers are willing to refer friends and family even on high-value items such as solar roofs and solar panels. Using their custom-generated referral link, customers who share with friends that make a purchase get $500 for each roof referral and $300 for each panel referral, while new customers get the same in discounts off their new solar purchases.

- When you refer a friend to **Stitch Fix**, an online styling and shopping service, you get a credit on your next order. The amount of the credit varies, so be sure to check your account's referrals page to see how much you can earn. It's an easy step to go from telling someone where you got your outfit to sending them a link to try it themselves, so pairing that with a compelling credit or discount makes this program successful.

HOW TO BUILD COMPANY AWARENESS AND GOODWILL

Have you ever heard people refer to themselves as "Apple people," "Nike people," or "Trader Joe's" people?

This is what brand awareness can do for a brand: embed itself into consumer lifestyles and purchase habits so that they don't have to think twice before becoming a customer—time and time again.

Brand awareness is, therefore, an indicator of a company's marketing strategy that consists of making the brand remembered and recognized.

The goal of brand awareness is to get users to associate a brand with the product category and think of it first, which increases the likelihood that they will choose it over the competition. The greater the brand awareness, the more familiar the public will become with your logo, your messages, and your products.

Awareness establishes that trust in the brand. When you put a proverbial face to your brand, consumers can more easily trust. Brand awareness efforts give your brand a personality and an outlet to be sincere, receive feedback, and tell a story. These are all ways we, as humans, build trust with each other. The relationship between humans and brands is no different.

At the same time, **"goodwill" is a strategic asset and a secret to future success that companies must cultivate and protect in order to compete more effectively**. This is truer today than at any other time in history. In particular, "goodwill" is the safety and safety net for brands facing more complex reputational risk challenges. In today's "always-on" world, combined with a news context of fact versus fiction, a brand plays a critical role in safeguarding and protecting market share, strength, and preference for all stakeholders and audiences. Increasingly, "goodwill" is the determining factor in whether a brand will make or break. "Goodwill" is the result of a solid reputation, strong customer relationships, and a proactive brand management culture. When all three are nurtured, the value of the brand asset is more effectively protected.

Awareness and goodwill are therefore fundamental aspects that any company that wants to endure over time and be successful must take on and deal with in a comprehensive manner. Consumers now expect much more from companies than just good products. Companies must now set an example and act in accordance with the values of an increasingly informed and aware society. The key to success is to be consistent and try to enhance the image of your brand in the minds of your target audience. For this, our Harmonic Messaging is an essential strategy that will help us to transmit the values, mission, and vision of our company in an efficient and harmonious way.

A Proactive Strategy—from Brand Awareness through Loyalty to "Goodwill"

Goodwill begins with the value of a company, product, or service name. Pay attention to the degree of familiarity and awareness, plus the associations that have been invested in the brand name. This is the basis of reputation and the creation of potential demand for the brand. Once an audience has been established for a brand and products, services or values are delivered through consistent, relevant, and distinctive experiences, a brand begins to build "goodwill." At the core of this concept are consistency, satisfaction, and credibility. A brand must be consistent in delivering reliable customer satisfaction through its products, services, or communications so that the brand promise can be easily discerned, anticipated, and delivered.

For employees, a brand's performance standards should be tied to the physical manifestation of the brand experience and alignment with the brand's distinctive values, aesthetics, and customer-centric culture. Employees are representatives of the brand and, therefore, along with the product, are the "front line" of brand performance. The more distinctive, differentiated, and desired a brand is, the greater the demand for it among its audience. When a brand is managed for positive and effective awareness, consideration, and purchase, the net effect is to create positive "goodwill." The brand and its marketing, communications, and sales become more effective in attracting new customers, employees, and investors or partners because its positive reputation precedes it. The "goodwill" that results from ongoing interactions and expectations further fuels brand satisfaction and reinforces the consumer's or customer's interest in the brand and their continued purchase. Thus, "goodwill" in the sense of reputation is an **intangible asset that exists because of historical performance, reputation, and associations**. Brand managers' decisions that reinforce positive perceptions and public expectations are the means by which "goodwill" is protected and enhanced.

The true test of a brand and its reputation is often cited in times of crisis. It can take years to develop and nurture a brand's reputation, but all it takes is a single crisis to test the true strength of the brand. Therefore, in developing a "brand first" and "goodwill" strategy, it is wise for leadership and brand management to consider how brand reputation can be leveraged in times of crisis or challenge. In cases of crisis such as that which occurred with Samsung and its "exploding" phones a few years ago, steps had to be taken to make substantial, tangible changes and respond to consumer demand for accountability. The brand was expected to act and their "goodwill" with consumers gave them the opportunity to resolve the crisis. By addressing the core elements of their brands and the expectations of their brand promises, consumers will be able to judge whether the brand is worthy of forgiveness and future business.

Purpose, Vision, and Values Determine All Aspects of the Company's Experience and Product or Service

A company's purpose and values and its way of seeing the world influence the perceptions of consumers, employees, and potential customers. For millennials, there is a demand to know a brand's convictions and ethos as a company and, in particular, the brand's views on issues and concerns related to people, communities, and the environment disproportionately to the brand's views on commercial success and profitability. The degree to which a brand leverages this content and uses it to guide decision-making on all aspects of products, services, and employee management is often the difference in creating affinity and preference for brands across categories.

For a brand to be successful, there are a number of factors that must contribute to its commercial viability and success in the face of differentiation and distinction. One of the most important is the brand's ability to generate "goodwill" based on its guiding philosophy, commitment to ethical and transparent communication, employee rights, and consumer rights. In all aspects of business, when a company focuses on company values and builds a business case that is profitable for all stakeholders, the brand receives greater prestige and preference over the competition. This is especially important when there is a crisis of confidence in product or service performance, or when values are called upon to determine what is "right" and what is good for all stakeholders, not just the commercial success of the brand as a company. Goodwill is largely influenced by consumer expectations, shaped by a brand's purpose, vision, and values.

Brand Awareness Is the Secret to Leveraging "Goodwill" in Times of Crisis

Good brand awareness is undoubtedly one of the company's most important assets when dealing with a crisis or expanding the business. The ability to draw on previously established "goodwill" and "reputation" in times of challenge, disruption, or disappointment is critical to understanding how the brand's strongest advocates and loyalists can be expected to "forgive" and "defend" the brand. Brand fans or repeat customers are a brand's most fervent believers and defenders, and it is these most passionate supporters who represent the true test of a brand's strength. "Goodwill" among brand advocates can be created by using proven marketing techniques to help defend and support a brand in times of crisis or reputational challenges.

Here are some other valuable things that come from positive brand awareness and goodwill:

- Higher prices due to higher perceived value
- Higher stock price
- The ability to expand the business through product or service line extensions
- Increased social impact due to brand equity

Creating brand awareness and goodwill:

- **Be human**. When you meet a new friend, what do you like to discover about them? I like to know what their hobbies are, their passions, their likes and dislikes. I also look at how they talk, what they like to talk about, and what things excite them. These are the traits that your brand should determine and promote about itself. To make an impact on your audience, you have to define yourself as more than just a company that sells things. How else would you define yourself? What words would you use if you had to introduce your brand to a new friend?

- **Socialize**. If you only try to connect with others when you're trying to make a sale or get support, you won't be known beyond a business with singular intent. To create awareness and project goodwill, you have to be social. Post on social media about things unrelated to your product or services. Interact with your audience by asking questions, commenting on posts, or retweeting or sharing content you like. *Treat your social accounts as if you were a person trying to make friends, not a company trying to make money.*
- **Tell a story**. Storytelling is an incredibly powerful marketing tactic, whether you're marketing products or promoting your brand. Why? Because it gives your audience something real to hold on to. Crafting a narrative around your brand humanizes it and gives it depth. And by weaving this narrative into your marketing, your brand is inherently marketed along with your products or services. What should your narrative be about? Anything—as long as it's true. It can be the story of your founder, the story of how your company came up with its first product idea,

or the story of the little engine that was able to make it in this big world. People like to hear stories about others. Authenticity is impactful and can be a big boost to brand awareness and goodwill.

- **Sponsor events**. Event sponsorships are a surefire way to get your brand out to hundreds, thousands, or millions of people who likely belong to your target audience. From banners to flyers to water bottles, your brand name will be everywhere if you sponsor an event.

By associating your company's brand with an event or location that your target audience views positively, you are shaping attitudes and helping to generate a positive reaction to your brand. Ultimately, your goal is to improve your target audience's perception of your brand. This happens in a number of ways, including:

- *"Good Neighbor"*: Local sponsorships are especially effective at generating consumer goodwill because they see the sponsoring company investing in the community and contributing to the economic growth of the community. This is especially true if a local event cannot be held without sponsorship support.
- *Differentiation from the competition*: Sponsorships can differentiate your company from the competition. What can customers expect from your company that sets it apart from others? How can you demonstrate that difference through a

branded sponsorship? Working through these questions is part of a solid sponsorship strategy.

- *Enhancing relationships*: Sponsorships often offer companies perks such as VIP seating, private receptions, exclusive tickets, etc. Leverage these perks to build relationships with key employees, key customers and prospects, and referral partners.

  Think of Red Bull. Red Bull is an energy drink, and without any brand awareness efforts, we would consider it simply an energy drink. But, fortunately, Red Bull took their marketing to the extreme—literally—by sponsoring extreme sporting events like cliff diving and motocross. They also sponsor athletes. Now, we intrinsically associate Red Bull with daring and adventure . . . and believe that if we drink it, we can be the same.
- *Have a plan for crisis situations*. Crisis management is not about weathering the storm. In fact, navigating these turbulent waters requires more than battening down the hatches or climbing into a lifeboat. Today's challenges demand that the problem be addressed. Companies must first build the infrastructure and tools to steer the waters. If done right, brands can even emerge from incidents in a stronger position. Getting forgiveness from customers and the general public is no longer a luxury that can be left for a "rainy day." From cybersecurity to social media rumors, the risks continue to grow. Threats to a company's reputation will come faster, harder, and much

more frequently. Creating "goodwill" reserves aligned with a purpose-driven, values-driven business plan can help reduce risks and build brand awareness. In an age when reputational risk is regular, developing strategic reservoirs of "goodwill" is defining the difference between the rise, fall, and future of brands. If a brand isn't investing in these reputational reserves, they may find the next crisis is the last for the brand.

HOW TO SEEK OUT NEW BUSINESS OPPORTUNITIES

Detecting market opportunities is essential for the company's growth and survival. Opportunities are factors that contribute to your growing success. They are usually external and include such things as:

- Economic trends
- Market trends
- Changing or expanding customer base
- Changes in government or industry regulations
- Changes in partnerships or relationships with suppliers, competitors, etc.
- New or changing funding prospects (e.g., increased subsidies)

One of the best ways to identify new business opportunities is to conduct a SWOT analysis. SWOT analysis is one of the most popular strategic analysis tools. It focuses on four key factors that affect your business:

- Strengths
- Weaknesses
- Opportunities
- Threats facing your company

A SWOT analysis often provides you with valuable information about your company. It can help you identify new opportunities and prospects that you can potentially exploit. For example, if the SWOT analysis shows that your opportunities lie in changing market trends, you can respond by introducing new products, changing the pricing of existing products, adapting your advertising, or adding value to the customer experience.

In addition to using a SWOT analysis, to detect new business prospects, you can also:

- **Segment your customers**: Divide your customer base into smaller groups that share common characteristics, such as age, gender, location or lifestyle, attitude, or buying habits. This allows you to analyze the demand for your products or services and target each segment with specific marketing, promotions, and offers, which will ultimately help you seize new business opportunities.
- **Listen to your customers**: When talking to your customers, listen to what they say about your industry, products, and services. What are their most frequently asked questions, experiences, frustrations, reactions, and complaints? This valuable customer information will help you identify key business opportunities to expand and develop your current products and services.

- **Analyze your buying situation**: Examine distribution channels, payment methods, and other purchase-related factors to understand how your customers buy your products or services. Then consider how you can improve them or offer alternatives to attract new customers to your business.
- **Analyze your competition**: Research existing companies in the market to understand their value proposition and competitive advantage. Establish your unique selling point to differentiate yourself from your competitors. Identify what appeals to your customers and promote it.
- **Examine other markets**: Exporting to other countries can open up new opportunities. Carefully consider what the market is like. To increase your chances of success, research competitors, local customs, and potential demand for your products or services.

Also consider exploiting other types of business opportunities. For example, you can:

- Franchise your business
- Buy an existing business
- Find a distributor to increase your market share
- Explore licensing, supply chain agreements, etc.

Whatever growth opportunities for your business you consider, always keep the big picture of your brand in mind and make data-driven decisions to ensure the survival of your business in case something goes wrong.

CHAPTER 4 WORKSHEET

BUSINESS DEVELOPMENT

To begin considering the growth of our business we must first make an exercise of self-knowledge and, for this, we must understand where we are with respect to our competition. Let's start by understanding this through a few small exercises. Try to answer the following questions:

1. Who are your competitors?
   - List all the companies in your area offering the same services to the same niche target market.
   - List the most well-known of those competitors.

....

....

....

....

....

....

....

....

....

....

....

....

....

....

....

....

....

....

....

....

....

2. What are your competitors' marketing strategies?
   - List all of the marketing strategies used by these competitors.
   - List the most successful of those strategies.
   - List the least successful of those strategies.

....

....

....

....

....

....

....

....

3. What opportunities are your competitors missing?
   - List the services you offer that your competition does not.
   - List the services where you exceed the services of your competition.

....

....

....

....

....

....

....

....

....

....

....

....

....

....

....

....

....

....

…………………………………………………………………………

…………………………………………………………………………

…………………………………………………………………………

…………………………………………………………………………

…………………………………………………………………………

…………………………………………………………………………

…………………………………………………………………………

…………………………………………………………………………

…………………………………………………………………………

4. What opportunities am I missing?
    - List any additional information that you need to learn about your competition.
    - List potential reasons that your target market would choose the competition.
    - List ways that you can better reach your target market.

…………………………………………………………………………

…………………………………………………………………………

…………………………………………………………………………

…………………………………………………………………………

…………………………………………………………………………

…………………………………………………………………………

…………………………………………………………………………

....

....

....

....

....

....

....

....

....

....

....

....

....

....

....

....

....

You may have already done one for your business plan, but it is convenient at this point to perform a SWOT analysis to be aware of our opportunities and possibilities for expanding our business. Complete the following chart thinking of all those points that can be useful:

STRENGTHS	WEAKNESSES
OPPORTUNITIES	THREATS

Now is a great time to work on developing your outreach strategies. Consider these statements, questions, and components as you begin to plan your local outreach activities.

What is your organization hoping to accomplish through its outreach efforts?

....

....

....

....

....

....

....

....

How effective are current programs and services that address the problem in your community/target area?

....

....

....

....

....

....

....

....

....

What has been done by other organizations that have conducted campaigns on this issue? How effective were the campaigns?

....

....

....

....

....

....

....

....

Who are some of your potential partners?

....

....

....

....

....

....

....

....

....

How will you evaluate if your campaign is effective?

....

....

....

....

....

....

....

....

Do you have the resources to fulfill this strategy? (Think about your current partnerships and alliances.)

....

....

....

....

....

....

....

....

....

Current outreach activities of my organization:

1. --
   ----
2. --
   ----
3. --

Future outreach activities of my organization:

1. --
----
2. --
----
3. --

Challenges and barriers to community outreach:

....

....

....

....

....

....

....

....

....

Opportunities for increased community outreach:

....

....

....

....

....

....

....

....

Primary purpose of my outreach activities:

a) Awareness
b) Marketing Advocacy
c) Community Engagement
d) Other:______________

Are there particular individuals who have credibility or power over the target audience? If so, identify them:

....

....

....

....

....

....

....

....

....

....

....

....

....

....

....

Advocates are a great type of partnership to build customer numbers. List your potential referral sources. This list could include current customers, past customers, leads that may not have closed, industry leaders, your vendors, etc. This will give you a solid footing to start with.

....

....

....

....

....

....

....

....

....

....

....

....

....

Getting a partner can be one of the best ways to expand your business. However, it is a difficult decision that should be made with caution. Here are some questions that will help you make a wiser decision.

VALUES: Do you share similar values? Will you both fundamentally be moving in the same directions? Do you both want the same or complementary things? What things do you want that might be at cross purposes with each other?

....

....

....

....

....

....

....

....

....

....

....

....

....

....

....

CONFLICT: How does your prospective partner deal with conflict? Is this a match for your style? In times of stress will your partner stay the course or cut and run? How have they dealt with conflict in their past personal and business relationships? What clues are you able to uncover that reveal the real story?

………………………………………………………………………

………………………………………………………………………

………………………………………………………………………

………………………………………………………………………

………………………………………………………………………

………………………………………………………………………

………………………………………………………………………

………………………………………………………………………

………………………………………………………………………

………………………………………………………………………

………………………………………………………………………

………………………………………………………………………

………………………………………………………………………

………………………………………………………………………

………………………………………………………………………

………………………………………………………………………

………………………………………………………………………

WORK ETHIC: What type of hours will this person work? How much work will they put into those hours? How effective are they? What is their work style and can you live with it?

INTEGRITY: Do you trust this person? Is that trust based on real data or an emotional connection? How has this person behaved in their past? Does this person consistently meet their commitments, big or small? Will this person do what's right, especially when it isn't convenient or profitable?

....

....

....

....

....

....

....

....

....

....

....

....

....

....

....

....

....

DEVIL'S ADVOCATE: Why shouldn't you partner with this person? What dangers could you face if you move forward with the deal? How might you feel in a few years' time if you move ahead in this arrangement that you've been ignoring or refusing to allow yourself to see?

....

....

....

....

....

....

....

....

....

....

....

....

....

....

....

....

....

DISAGREEMENT: What happens if you and your partners reach an impasse . . . an irreconcilable difference on a fundamentally important issue? How will you handle it? Will one of you have the final say? Or will you instead have the last resort be a carefully thought through buy-sell agreement?

....

....

....

....

....

....

....

....

....

....

....

....

....

....

....

....

....

DEBT: What happens if any of the partners becomes financially insolvent and declares bankruptcy? Will you have to take on that partner's creditors as your new partners? (Usually, in the case of bankruptcy, the economic interest of the insolvent partner will revert back to the other partners, or, at the very least, be strictly limited to the economic interest and not any voting or controlling rights. This protects members of the partnership.)

DIVORCE: Let's say you're a partner with Sally. But she and her husband Jim get a divorce and in the settlement Jim gets half of Sally's interest in your partnership. Do you really want to be forced to take Jim into your partnership? You need to decide upfront how you want to handle this contingency.

....

....

....

....

....

....

....

....

....

....

....

....

....

....

....

....

....

DISABILITY: What happens if one of the partners is hurt and is no longer able to contribute time and talent to the partnership? How will this affect their ownership interest and the way profits are split?

....

....

....

....

....

....

....

....

....

....

....

....

....

....

....

....

....

....

....

CHAPTER 5

HOW SALES AND MARKETING CAN WORK TOGETHER FOR A HARMONIOUS RELATIONSHIP

If sales and marketing aren't aligned, you fundamentally have a broken forecasting process. That's not good for anybody.

—Jon Miller, Marketo

No two departments are more intertwined than those that create the "why you should buy a product" messages and those that are in charge of selling it. That's why "sales" and "marketing" are often expressed in a single phrase: Smarketing.

However, despite sharing a common goal—revenue generation—the relationships between these two intrinsically linked departments are often far from harmonious. Cultural differences and misunderstood roles can even cause these teams to end up as adversaries rather than partners. So much so that, according to IDC, 10 percent of company revenue can be lost due to this lack of alignment.

With the modern marketplace changing and so much of the buyer's journey taking place online, it's time for these two departments to come together, celebrate their differences, and work together to gain a long-term advantage. **Because when sales and marketing are aligned, the rewards can be significant: up to 36 percent higher retention rates, 28 percent higher sales rates, and 208 percent more revenue generated from marketing efforts, according to Marketing Profs**.

A successful sales and marketing partnership shares, in many ways, similar characteristics to a good marriage and, with a little effort on both sides, can lead to a productive and happy long-term union.

WHY THE FRICTION?

Frankly, it shouldn't be that hard, right? Sales and marketing work in the same company. They share the same business objectives. They market and sell the same products. In some organizations, they even report to the same manager or belong to the same group. They should be on the same team. Well, the devil is in the details.

Fundamentally, sales and marketing differ in:

- **Different department objectives**: Sales focuses on revenue, while marketing focuses on demand generation and brand recognition, or both.
- **Different long-term and short-term priorities**:

Sales is in the trenches focusing on monthly and quarterly installments, while marketing has to focus on massive brand awareness and facilitating prospects through the entire purchase funnel, which takes longer than a month or a quarter.

- **Different resource and support allocation**: Sales processes and methodology are more linear, while the buying cycle goes back and forth between the top and middle of the funnel before customers make the final purchase decision. Sales resource allocation is based on sales processes, while marketing outreach tends to be based on the channel or buying journey.

If these concerns and differences are not discussed and addressed between sales and marketing in a timely manner, misalignment and friction will continue.

So you may not be able to end the war, but there are ways to call a truce and extend some olive branches so that the company can benefit from a better functioning "smarketing" machine. When marketing and sales work in harmony, the result is increased sales, with shorter cycle times and higher margins, and increased customer satisfaction. The alignment of marketing and sales is a critical factor for the company to achieve higher performance of its sales force and sales function.

The buyer's journey has changed. This change in the buyer's journey requires digital marketers to create content that captures leads in the awareness phase, nurtures them, and qualifies them until they are ready to move to sales.

An annual study conducted by the Content Marketing Institute[3]—which interviewed hundreds of professionals from both departments, those who are aligned and those who are not—sheds light on several of the most common problems that arise in the harmonization of these two pillars of companies.

Survey respondents indicate that their marketing and sales teams collaborate the most on "content topics." However, collaboration declines on "content types" (38 percent say they rarely or never collaborate on this topic). As we can see, not often do departments collaborate on agreeing how and when to use content, as well as analyzing the effectiveness of the content. Thus, if there is no collaboration, money could be wasted creating the wrong content and making our communication strategy unharmonized and losing most of its effectiveness.

Neither marketing nor sales can achieve greatness alone. They need each other and can leverage each other's core competencies to achieve the organization's goals. Here are four steps to improve sales and marketing alignment:

1. *Identify weaknesses*

Both sales and marketing are working to grow the company. Both want more customers, more brand awareness, and more profits. Although each team takes a different path, ultimately they are all going in the same direction. The first step to improvement always starts

---

[3] https://contentmarketinginstitute.com/2021/04/content-marketing-help-sales-research/.

with defining the problems. **Both sales and marketing management should discuss areas to improve the alignment of both departments.**

During this discussion, it is important to lay the groundwork for future initiatives. Beyond identifying the problems facing sales and marketing, be sure to start with next steps to solve the problems, create a cross-functional vision, designate roles, and build a process for moving forward. Some useful questions to lay the foundations of the groundwork for collaboration may include:

- What objections are you getting when it comes time to close the sale?
- What are some of the reasons people choose our company?
- What are the most frequently asked questions you hear when making the sale?
- Do people prefer to meet virtually, by phone, or in person?
- What can we (the marketing department) do to better qualify your leads?
- What sales materials do you need to make your job easier?

This allows your company's sales and marketing departments to work together in harmony. The marketing team can repurpose content that answers the sales team's questions and create content for the website, social media, tradeshows, email campaigns, newsletters, and videos that respond to objections and inquiries.

2. *Agree on terminology, metrics, and objectives*

Marketing and sales must define and agree on terminology. This process helps extinguish the debate over lead quality and holds each department accountable. This process will also improve your reporting capabilities, as you will be able to clearly recognize and track the metrics that matter. Here are some questions to consider:

- What markets are we targeting?
- What criteria define a marketing qualified lead (MQL)?
- What criteria define a sales qualified lead (SQL)?
- What are our conversion goals (e.g., leads, sales, revenue)?

3. *Use technology to improve the lead handoff process*

There are a variety of marketing and sales automation tools available to improve sales and marketing coordination. Marketing automation tools, such as Eloqua, HubSpot, and Pardot, help with lead generation, lead scoring, and streamlining the lead-to-sales handoff process. Sales automation technology and CRM systems such as Keap, Salesforce, and SugarCRM are designed to help drive sales productivity, increase visibility into sales performance, and manage leads.

These tools are useful on their own, but the integration of sales and marketing platforms is where these technologies really shine. Integrated tools are designed to reliably synchronize leads from your website with your CRM dashboard.

In this way, **marketers can help nurture leads, shortening the sales cycle, while sales can use the context**

generated by marketing to have more relevant sales conversations. A closed-loop system moves leads seamlessly through the sales cycle, creating a smoother handoff and a more consistent customer experience.

Integrated technology also offers the opportunity to report on the entire funnel and measure ROI. Marketing and sales can see the entire customer lifecycle, from the first interaction to the most recent conversion.

4. *Communicate and collaborate*

The two essential aspects of successful sales and marketing alignment are communication and collaboration. Consistent communication and collaboration reduce the chances of misunderstandings, lost leads, reporting blind spots, and missed opportunities. Here are some tips to help point you in the right direction for productive communication and collaboration:

- **Meet frequently**. Set consistent days and times to meet and review activities, goals and challenges, and share information. Depending on how your organization is structured, this meeting may include the sales and marketing teams or the leaders of each. **Make meetings consistent and purposeful.** Don't meet for the sake of meeting.
- **Provide feedback**. You will never know how to improve or what is working if you are not open to giving and receiving constructive feedback. Allow people, both sales and marketing, to offer feedback, understanding that everyone is trying to achieve common goals.

- **Lean on data**. Data can be used to better understand sales and marketing performance. Reports can reveal what's working well and what needs improvement, remove emotion from the conversation, and drive strategies based on unbiased information. Data can also provide a strong argument for ROI and give insights into future allocation.
- **Encourage an "all as one" approach**. Sales and marketing are united around a common goal and respect each other's role in achieving it. While they may not always agree on everything, they are on the same page when it comes to the big picture.
- **Share resources**. Your marketing team may have created a library of valuable content: blog posts, case studies, white papers, tip sheets, product web pages, and more. But creating marketing assets is only half the battle. Give your content real legs by leveraging the sales team.

For better or worse . . . there's no denying that it's easier for sales and marketing to be in sync when things are going well, content is working, leads are flourishing, and customers are buying. It's when times are tough, or companies are in a period of change, that relationships are really tested.

Positive communication, trust, and respect are imperative to prevent a "them and us" culture from reemerging and to avoid accusatory finger-pointing. To weather the storm, a bond of trust and cohesion must be created.

Let's face it, no marriage is trouble-free, but if you do

the above to the best of your ability, you will weather the difficulties and bumps to work as an aligned team, achieving joint goals, meeting customer needs, and driving growth.

Sales Enablement: The Key to Your Company's Commercial Harmonization

In short, **sales enablement is a system that aims to create a scalable and repeatable sales process by creating an ideal model for the sales team to achieve maximum performance**. Therefore, its function is also to align marketing and sales strategies, explore all that the product or service has to offer, and optimize the commercial approach. A tool that provides the marketing department with accurate information to provide the sales team with the materials they need to maximize sales.

The truth is that there is no unanimity when it comes to defining it, but the most important thing is to understand what it consists of, and there is a broad consensus.

The mechanical engineering company, Gartner, defines sales enablement as "the activities, systems, processes and information that support and promote knowledge-based sales interactions with customers and prospects."

The global management consulting company, McKinsey, speaks of "processes for redesigning, automating and optimizing sales support resources."

In short, it's about **providing your sales team with the best tools and content so they can sell faster and more efficiently. Doing more with less, as today's market demands.**

The data provided by the Content Marketing Institute study shows the importance of adopting a sales enablement strategy to align and harmonize our business objectives. Today in the United States, approximately 38 percent of small companies have adopted sales enablement, as well as 55 percent of medium-sized companies and 68 percent of large companies. Of these, 75 percent reported significant contributions to their business outreach.

In addition, according to a HubSpot survey involving professionals working in commercial teams who already have a sales enablement professional, the main actions involving them are:

- Strategy development
- Creation of materials
- Choice of tools
- Commercial training
- Performance analysis
- New channel integration
- Optimization of sales operations
- Coaching practices
- Better recruitment of new members

Why This Boom of Sales Enablement?

> *"Do more for less." If there were a tagline for sales in the past couple of years, that might be it.*
>
> —McKinsey & Company

Very simple: it is the best resource for your sales team to face the challenges and new trends of today's market, and it is precisely these new trends that are forcing companies to rethink how they sell.

No wonder, then, that according to Google Trends, searches for "sales enablement" have increased by 20 percent in the last year. Consumers don't want more of the same, more of what they have traditionally been offered. The enormous amount of information available on the internet, product comparisons, and opinions of other customers provide them with greater knowledge, a higher degree of demand, and a greater awareness of their power when choosing among so many competitors fighting for their attention.

For all these reasons, the profile of the salesperson with a superficial knowledge of the product and the market is no longer valid in the face of this increasingly informed and demanding customer.

McKinsey[4] states that companies that manage to implement a sales enablement solution experience productivity increases of between 20 percent and 30 percent and sustained annual growth of between 5 percent and 10 percent in some cases.

What Characterizes Sales Enablement?

So . . . anything that improves sales can be considered sales enablement? Yes, but its strength lies in the fact that it is a thoughtful, well-planned process aimed at optimizing everything that directly or indirectly has to do with sales.

In other words, it is not a matter of taking measures that may seem right here and there. Sales enablement implies a perfectly designed strategy with the following characteristics:

---

[4] https://www.mckinsey.com/business-functions/marketing-and-sales/our-insights/looking-beyond-technology-to-drive-sales-operations.

- *A clear objective*: Provide your sales team with the resources they need to sell more efficiently, whether from a technological point of view, relevant content, or information, among others.
- *Customer-centric*: The customer is the center of everything. Sales enablement is not so much about sales as it is about the customer. The objective of the previous point is not to offer your salesperson an infallible closing technique, but rather resources that allow him/her to capture the attention and interest of the target audience. In reality, you offer your salesperson what the customer wants or needs.
- *Training and development of the sales team*: Your sales force must know how to apply and get the most out of all the resources you are going to put at their disposal. That's why training plays a key role. To do this, you must combine traditional learning methods with other tools that make training a continuous process for your sales force.
- *Ease of use*: Sales enablement solutions accompany your sales force at all times and promote continuous learning, and therefore must not only be always at their fingertips but must also be agile in use and intuitive in learning to encourage their use on a daily basis.
- *Control and monitoring of use*: If your team does not use the tools you make available to them, all effort will be in vain. You must be

able to keep track of the resources used and promote those that are most beneficial to your sales team. Keeping track of the tools that are being used will allow you to know if some of them are or are not useful, ask why they are not being used and, eventually, replace them with others that better serve your sales team.

How Does Sales Enablement Work?

Sales enablement platforms work mainly as a content manager where you can upload your products or services. But the advantages go far beyond that. In addition to presenting the elements of the catalog in an attractive way, it allows you to update it based on usage metrics that you get from your own customers.

Let's look at an example of use in a company:

1. The marketing team creates the contents of the virtual catalog.
2. The sales staff presents the company's products or services thanks to the virtual catalog, either remotely or in person with the help of a tablet.
3. The customer interacts with the catalog, selecting those products or services that suit them best.
4. The Sales enablement platform generates usage metrics that help the marketing team to optimize content and presentation. At the same time, the metrics are of great use to the company's management. As the information is generated in real-time, decision-making and implementation of improvements can be accelerated considerably.

5. Thanks to continuous catalog improvements, sales conversion time is reduced.

Creating Content that Enables Sales

Creating content for your brand that is in line with your buyer personas is a crucial part of sales enablement, and can make your sales process decisive. When it comes to sales enablement solutions, the types of content you create can have a major effect on the number of sales you close. A survey conducted by DemandMetric[5] provides some examples of what can be considered sales enablement content, including:

- Informative blog posts
- Case studies
- Customer testimonials
- Interactive content
- Printed materials
- Email campaigns

From a sales content management standpoint, digital content is a highly valuable aspect of any effective online sales funnel. These materials are developed to keep prospects moving through the sales funnel and connected to the sales process.

However, it is important to note that content created for sales enablement is often different from content created for content marketing purposes. According to Seismic[6], content created for the conversion and closing stages of

[5] https://www.demandmetric.com/content/sales-enablement-infographic.

[6] https://seismic.com/company/blog/the-difference-between-content-marketing-and-sales-enablement/.

the sales funnel is classified as sales enablement content, while content created to attract leads and convert them into prospects is content for marketing purposes.

When a marketing and sales team is aligned on the types of content created for sales enablement versus those created for content marketing purposes, a sales team can use well-placed drops across multiple touchpoints to make the final conversion from lead to loyal customer.

The following list highlights the eight essential content types you can use as high-quality sales enablement solutions:

1. *Competitive research and analysis materials*: A high-quality competitive analysis document educates sales professionals on how they can better persuade a high-potential prospect to make the last step in the online sales funnel. Competitive research and analysis content allows brands to gain insight into how their competition is connecting with their target audience while highlighting areas where they are lacking.
2. *Case studies and other customer-centric content*: Customer-centric content demonstrates the difficulties and challenges your target audience faces, which guides salespeople to share content and information that shows how your product or service can be the high-value solution they've been looking for. This type of customer-centric content can be provided to sales teams in many forms, such as case studies, video testimonials, or written customer

recommendations. Ideally, this type of content should communicate the value your company provides to your customers.

3. *Blog posts*: While content marketing and sales enablement materials are developed for different uses, some content marketing materials, such as informative blog posts, can be used during the later stages of an online sales funnel. As sales enablement tools, blog posts are high-value references that can educate sales professionals and be used by them to nurture leads and close a sale.
4. *E-books*: While traditionally used for content marketing purposes early in the sales process, gated content such as e-books and white papers are valuable materials for both content marketers and sales professionals. These comprehensive documents and resources often contain statistics and educational information on how a brand's service or product will provide the solution a prospect needs.
5. *Social media content*: Social media channels provide a high-converting platform for both content marketers and sales professionals. The messaging aspects of these channels are especially important sales enablement solutions, as they provide a foundation for meaningful prospect engagement. For example, sales teams can send links to previous social media content that followers have interacted well with.
6. *Onboarding content*: Training and onboarding materials developed for sales professionals are

critical sales training tools. These documents not only provide new sales team members with information about the company but demonstrate the ideal voice and tone to use during customer interactions. When developing these sales training materials, be sure to include content such as your company's mission and values, and tips on how sales professionals can successfully use the pre-developed content to their advantage.

What Benefits Can Sales Enablement Bring to Companies?

Now that you know how to apply sales enablement, let's take a look at some of the benefits it can bring:

- *Visibility in tasks*: Many companies are constantly looking to optimize their commercial activities until they realize that they have no idea how to do it. This happens precisely because of the lack of daily monitoring of results; objectives should be achieved on a daily basis and not on a monthly basis.

  Therefore, the first step is to make the entire sales process visible by tracking the activities of all team members, reps, as well as SDRs and managers.

  How many leads do SDRs convert into opportunities?

  Of these opportunities, how many do reps convert into customers?

  How long does it take to qualify and service these leads?

What is the average ticket for each salesperson?

What is the satisfaction level of the customers who go through this process?

To answer these questions, the sales enablement professional needs to closely monitor these activities.

- *Applied sales methodology*: Having a business methodology is an excellent way to transform ineffective activities into a structural sales process that salespeople must follow to achieve their objectives.

  It is important to remember that the sales methodology should not be limited to just a process recorded in a Google Drive document, but should be an integral and daily part of the business process and one that defines the path to success for salespeople. If your business team is not using a methodology, your company is certainly not making money, even if it is in the green.

- *Training sessions*: Although the sales team may have common pains and difficulties, it is also necessary to take into account the individual performance of each salesperson. That's why so many sales methodologies involve training the team, but it doesn't stop there.

  In addition to training, it is also necessary to identify the weaknesses of each member, since a salesperson who is not doing his job well compromises not only his individual objective but also the objective of the company linked to him. For this reason, post-training follow-up must be constant and periodic, as these points can be improved.

- *Alignment between marketing and sales*: Marketing and sales are two departments that are intrinsically connected; after all, while one develops campaigns and actions to generate increasingly qualified leads, the other tries to contact them and convert them into customers.

For entrepreneurs looking to help improve sales team success, aligning content creation with the immediate needs of sales professionals can help streamline the process for all parties involved. The best type of sales enablement content serves the good of the business by enabling salespeople to succeed in their efforts.

A comprehensive sales training approach that incorporates different types of assets is the key to better enable your sales team to win. If you are just starting out, begin with one of these elements and then fill in the gaps over time. If you already have a solid sales training program in place, look for where your sales team continues to struggle and identify gaps you can fill with these sales training materials.

> *True alignment requires integrating into one, cohesive customer journey—facilitated by extraordinary digital content—distributed and delivered in a helpful way by insightful sales teams. True collaboration among the teams is critical.*
>
> —Robert Rose, CMI

CHAPTER 5 WORKSHEET

MAKE SALES AND MARKETING WORK TOGETHER

Your marketing and sales departments will need to work closely together to have a harmonious relationship. The exercises in this section will help you assess the current state of your organization to know where to focus your efforts first.

Aligning goals: Describe your current process for setting company goals and translating them into departmental goals. How clearly defined is this process? How well do employees at all levels of the organization understand it?

....

....

....

....

....

....

....

....

....

....

....

....

Describe the relationship between marketing goals and sales goals in your company. Do marketing and sales have shared goals or separate goals? How closely are their goals aligned?

Processes: Describe when and how leads get passed between marketing and sales. How well is this process understood by the members of both teams?

....

....

....

....

....

....

....

....

....

....

....

....

....

....

....

....

....

....

....

Describe any processes you have in place to align marketing and sales, such as regular meetings, reports, service-level agreements, etc. How effective are these processes?

....

....

....

....

....

....

....

....

....

....

....

....

....

....

....

....

....

....

....

Is everyone in marketing and sales going to attend every meeting, or will you need to have rotations and divisions to keep the group small? How frequently will these meetings occur? (Remember, the default is to start meeting every two weeks and then adjust as needed.)

....

....

....

....

....

....

....

....

....

....

....

....

....

....

....

....

....

....

Content: Describe the content creation process at your company (if any). Who is in charge of it? Who else is involved? How effective is it? If you don't have a defined process, describe any efforts your company has made to produce content.

Describe the way content is (or isn't) currently used in your sales process. Do salespeople use the content marketing creates? Are they able to find it when they need it?

....

....

....

....

....

....

....

....

....

....

....

....

....

....

....

....

....

....

....

Technology: Describe the marketing technology your company is currently using. Where do you store and organize your contacts? What tools do you use to create and distribute content? How is your website managed? What tools do you use to communicate with marketing leads? Do you have a marketing automation platform?

Describe the sales technology your company is currently using. How do you store and organize your contacts? How do you track the progress of individual sales? How do you report the performance of individual salespeople? Do you have any tools to automate or simplify your sales process? Do you have a CRM?

....
....
....
....
....
....
....
....
....
....
....
....
....
....
....
....
....
....
....
....
....
....

CONCLUSION

Throughout this book we have delved into several of the most important topics of any marketing and sales strategy to determine the steps to follow in order to have our instruments well-tuned for our great performance. The public is increasingly expectant and we cannot fail, or our song will be lost among the thousands of other failed songs that do not end up connecting with the audience.

First, we found out that in order to make our performance memorable, we must define what we want to convey, what our identity will be, and how we are going to connect with our audience. To do so, we have learned how to create a powerful brand identity, adopting strong values, mission, and vision that will be the pillar of all our performance. Knowing who we are, what we do, where we are going, and how we want to achieve it will be the fundamental basis to start building a harmonic strategy that will end up transforming into more profits, loyalty, and impact.

In the case of an orchestra, the composer and conductor work hand in hand to harmonize all the parts and ensure that all the members know and master the language and the instrument. In our company, we must do the same with each and every one of the parties involved, from the executive directors to the employees who deal directly with the customer, so that our message resonates in the same tone, at the same frequency. As we saw in the first chapter, it is extremely important that all employees are on the same page and involved in the consolidation and dissemination of our identity. They are our musicians and they must have all the facilities at our disposal to perform at the highest level.

Of course, even if we have the sheet, and our musicians know the notes, we must create coherence and consistency in our performance. It would make no sense for us to play classical music and advertise ourselves as a rap group and dress like a heavy metal band. Our message must be uniform and convey the same sensations regardless of the medium chosen for it. Therefore, we must try to harmonize all types of content or messages that are launched from the company, whether through advertising, social media campaigns, events, web, or billboards. Any medium we choose to communicate with our audience must be governed by joint criteria based on our corporate identity.

In addition to harmonizing our messages, we must also try to integrate and unite each of the steps of our audience or customers throughout their journey with us. In this way, through the AIDA model, we can know and understand our customer's journey to try to empathize more effectively and obtain better results for the company. To know how to play we must first learn to listen, and therefore, understanding what our customers want or expect from us is essential to create connections beyond the commercial that make our audience see us as a reference and trustworthy. In the end, we do not perform to make money, but to create valuable and unforgettable moments for our audience. **We must aspire to create satisfaction and happiness, and for that, our customers must be at the center of everything.**

When we have overcome stage fright and our audience

is satisfied with our performance, the logical step is to keep growing to send our message to many more people. We may have managed to fill small concert halls and have a small group of fans who don't miss a single one of our concerts. But let's be honest, every band wants to play at the Royal Albert Hall or Madison Square Garden one day. For this we need to invest time in perfecting a business development plan, as we have seen in Chapter 4. Looking for new partners, new business opportunities, commercial relationships and even investing in creating company awareness and goodwill, we can take our business to the next level, and who knows, maybe to become one of the big fish in a few years and finally play in one of the big stages that only a few have access to.

As in all families, and in many bands in history, differences can often get in the way of common goals. Confrontation between two or more band members could mean the band's demise and a long list of unpleasant situations that would leave our band in a rather embarrassing place in front of our audience. As far as business is concerned, we have found that two departments have historically had a slightly more difficult coexistence: marketing and sales. For our band to sound good, as we have been repeating throughout this book, all of its members must be cohesive and in harmony with each other. Harmonizing the relationship between sales and marketing is an arduous task but one that has great short and long-term benefits for any business strategy. Finding common ground and using strategies such as sales enablement can give us the peace of mind that our band will never part ways and that our records will be remembered for centuries to come.

If you've made it this far—first, thank you. I hope this guide has been helpful and has provided you with ideas to take your business to the next level. As you have seen, harmonizing our messages throughout our business structure is not necessarily complicated or unrealistic. However, the results achieved when all the elements of our company are united under the same strategy are truly overwhelming.

Secondly, if you want to learn more about Harmonic Messaging, I invite you to visit my website www.BonnieMauldin.com, where you will find much more content, case studies, worksheets, and other materials that will help you get the most out of your marketing and sales strategies.

Thank you and see you next time!

REFERENCES

Aaker, D., and Joachimsthaler, E. *Brand Leadership*. New York: The Free Press, 2000.

Bagozzi, R. P., and U. M. Dholakia. "Antecedents and Purchase Consequences of Customer Participation in Small Group Brand Communities." *International Journal of Research in Marketing* 23, no. 1 (2006): 45–61.

Baker, M. *Marketing Management and Strategy*. London: Macmillan Business, 2000.

Barnes, N. G., and C. Daubitz. "Time for Re-evaluation? Social Media and the 2016 Inc. 500." Center for Marketing Research, University of Massachusetts, 2017. http://www.umassd.edu/cmr/socialmedia-research/2017inc500/.

Bowersox, D. J., and M. B. Cooper. *Strategic Marketing Channel Management*. New York: McGraw Hill, 1992.

"Harmonic Definition & Meaning." *Dictionary.com*, Dictionary.com, https://www.dictionary.com/browse/harmonic.

Jack, F. *Successful Business*. New York: McGraw Hill, 2000.

Kotler, P., and Armstrong, G. *Marketing: An Introduction*. Fourth Edition. New Jersey: Prentice Hall, 1997.

McMartin, J. *Personality Psychology: A Student-Centered Approach*. Newbury Park, California: Sage Publications, 1995.

Peter, J. P., and Olson, J. J. *Consumer Behaviour and Marketing Strategy*. New York: Irwin, 1996.

Peterson, R. "Sales Enablement: Developing a Dynamic Capability." *Journal Of the Academy of Marketing Science* (2020).

Proctor, T. *Essentials of Marketing Research.* UK: Financial Times-Prentice Hall, 2000.

Van Auken, B. *The Brand Management Checklist.* London: Kogan Page, 2002.

Weilbacher, W. *Brand Marketing: Building Winning Brand Strategies that Deliver Value and Customer Satisfaction.* Lincolnwood, IL: NTC Publishing Group, 1993.

Weinreich, N. (s.f.). *What Is Social Marketing?* http://www.social-marketing.com/Whatis.html.

Ziethmal, Valarie, Mary Jo Bitner, and Dwayne Gremler. *Services Marketing: Integrating Customer Focus across the Firm.* New York: McGraw Hill, 2003.

ABOUT THE AUTHOR

Her motto is "from the bottom to the top" because Bonnie comes from humble beginnings, growing up in a poverty-stricken neighborhood with crime, drugs, and gang influence everywhere. She did not let the poor environment define her. Instead, she studied hard in school, worked hard at multiple jobs, and fought her way out poverty using faith in God, lifelong learning, music, and entrepreneurship.

Starting out with her sights set on a career in medicine and with a full academic scholarship to Wayne State University, Bonnie Mauldin majored in clinical laboratory science, garnering a coveted internship with the renowned immunologist, Dr. Stuart Rater, at the Karmanos Cancer Institute. When she worked in a major metropolitan hospital as a surgical assistant and in the core chemistry lab, Bonnie wished to have a greater, more impact in the health of others. It was there that Healthopia was born, a revolutionary health and wellness coaching business, which introduced Bonnie to the world of digital marketing.

With the business world quickly evolving to a technology, internet-driven marketing sphere, Bonnie diligently learned about web design, SEO, social media, and podcasting when Google and Facebook were brand new and gaining popularity. Ravenously devouring hours of study, workshops, and training wherever she could attain it, Bonnie built an online following which led to her role in the movie *The Inner Weigh* and the reception of book propositions from major publishers. *The Healthtopia Radio Show* grew in popularity and garnered several prominent celebrity interviews.

Now, Bonnie is the owner of one of Atlanta's leading marketing agencies, an author, and a leader in her community. She serves on the board of directors for several prominent business and nonprofit organizations. As a mentor, Bonnie has worked with hundreds of career professionals and entrepreneurs to establish, grow, and excel on the corporate career track and in business ownership. Through her consulting services, Bonnie has worked with hundreds of individuals to not just reach but soar past their perceived potential to acquire success they only dreamed of.

Bonnie actively leads seminars, workshops, and webinars for business organizations and schools. Her trainings cover all phases of the business development process and have led many business owners to increase their sales and profits with strong, quick results.

For information about marketing, consulting, training, speaking, or media appearances contact us at info@bonniemauldin.com and visit www.BonnieMauldin.com.

Please share your feedback about what you learned from Harmonic Messaging on social media, and write a review for us on Amazon to help others "make their brand, sales and marketing sing in harmony!"

Wishing you the very best . . .